From a Bundle of Rags

From a Bundle of Rags

An Autobiography

JIM BOWEN

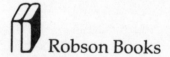

Robson Books

This Robson paperback edition first published in 1995

First published in Great Britain in 1994 by Robson Books
Ltd, Bolsover House, 5-6 Clipstone Street, London W1P 8LE

British Library Cataloguing in Publication Data
A catalogue record for this title is available from the British
Library

ISBN 0 86051 901 5 (hbk)
    0 86051 987 2 (pbk)

Printed in Great Britain by WBC Book Manufacturers Ltd,
Bridgend, Mid-Glamorgan

INTRODUCTION

'If you're not going to do any physical exercise, then how about writing a book? Exercise your mind for a change.'

Phyllis Bowen, Station House
10.30 a.m. 20 August 1993

1

The Stork in a Manilla Envelope

As a child, whenever we came across sheep in a field that were stamped with those coloured marks on their rear ends my mum and dad used to laugh and say the same thing had happened to me. I was stamped in a courtroom to prove I belonged to them.

You see, I haven't always been Jim Bowen of 'Bullseye'. Bowen is a name I chose with my wife when I entered the entertainment industry, before that I grew up as a Whittaker, and before that, on my first reported public appearance in 1938 at a children's home in Heswall, Liverpool, I was a Williams. It was as baby Peter Williams that I flew through the air into the arms of the lovely Annie Whittaker, an Olive Oyl lookalike with a heart of gold. Well, I like to imagine that I flew; in fact I was thrown at Annie, who caught me and decided to take me home. Not that she and her husband Joe had very much choice in the matter, but for me it really was a flying start in life – a moment that made me feel very special when my adoption was explained to me many years later. I like to think of it as my first experience of being in the right place at the right time.

The story of how I came to grow up as James Whittaker is one I loved to hear as a child and a tale which my adopted mother Annie never tired of telling. And it all began with a letter from Liverpool ...

Annie was a weaver at the Atlas Street mill in Clayton-le-Moors near Accrington in Lancashire. She was in charge of eight looms in the booming pre-war days of the East Lancashire cotton industry, which meant a long and noisy day of work that we'd call slave labour by modern standards. She was thin as a pin, with bright eyes that could dart as fast as the shuttles speeding to and fro across her looms, and she was proud of her skills. Her husband Joe was a setter at the Accrington Brick and Tile Company who came home from work covered in red brick dust, his sights set on better things.

A few years after their marriage they had learned that they were unable to have children. Annie was a natural mother but nature never blessed her with a child of her own, so they registered with an adoption society and hoped. Ten years went by, the springtime of her life was over and, as Annie approached forty, her dreams of a child running around their neat terraced house must have got pushed into a deep secret place inside her heart. Then came the day she loved to recall, when the postman delivered a certain letter.

'I remember that brown envelope falling through the letterbox,' she used to say. 'A letter was quite an occasion in those days, because we didn't get many, and I could see that it wasn't a bill, so my first reaction was to examine the postmark, out of curiosity, to see where it was from. In the light from the little window above the front door in the vestibule I could just make out a Liverpool postmark. Then I guessed it was from the adoption society. For a few seconds I daren't open it and just stood there clutching the manilla envelope.

'I went into the parlour to read the letter properly – there was plenty of light in there because it was a lovely, fresh spring morning, and what I read made my heart jump for joy. I was so excited! I read it again to be absolutely sure. The adoption society had written to say that me and your Dad should go to a children's home in Liverpool the very next day because there was a baby there waiting for us.'

I can imagine Mum sitting down to read the letter in the

calm of the 'best room' to give it a sense of occasion. She would have read it over slowly and pondered over the official language, as she did with all important letters, until she could have confidently believed what it said. Then, she told me, she became a whirlwind of action – she dashed through the house to pick up her purse from the kitchen, ran out into the street and all the way up the hill to the gates of the brickworks, where she grabbed the nearest dust-covered workshirt and shouted, 'Get Joe Whittaker! Get Joe Whittaker!'

My dad-to-be came to the gates, covered in dust and at first unable to fathom his wife's air of urgency.

'You've got to get the day off tomorrow, Joe.'

'Eh? You know I can't get an odd day off,' Dad was perplexed. 'What's the matter Annie?'

'We've got a baby. In Liverpool. You get the day off, I'll get the train tickets . . .' and away she ran again, without her coat, to the railway station.

Dad went straight to explain to the foreman, got the day off, had to tell everyone else why, then waited for the hooter signalling the end of the day's work to dash home and get his suit out of the wardrobe.

The following morning saw them on the first bus to Accrington, then a train to Blackburn, followed by another train to Liverpool. Mum had always thought the train journey to Accrington was a long one, but going to Liverpool was almost like going abroad. 'Your dad kept the train tickets in one pocket and the brown envelope with the letter in another,' she used to tell me. 'I was so excited I thought I would burst. At every single station, when the train stopped Dad would check that he still had the tickets and then take out the letter and check that it still said the same thing.'

She remembered holding on to his arm very tightly as they walked up the drive of the children's home. When they went inside a group of children came running to meet them, tugging at Annie's clothes and calling out, 'Hello Mum, hello Dad', offering their most winning smiles and hoping they'd be chosen to go home with them. But I was on my way, swaddled in ragged lengths of cloth and blankets in the arms of a large woman wearing a gleaming white apron and a high starched headdress – probably a nurse, but Mum thought she looked like a nun or possibly an angel.

'There's your bundle of rags,' said the nurse, and threw me across to Annie.

My mum said she was only about three feet away but it felt like fifty yards. She had to unravel my wrappings and push back layers of cloth to find my face under the bundle of rags, while Dad handed over the letter, which by now looked as if it had had an affair with a Dalmatian.

I remember all these romantic details because this was like hearing the story of my conception – in an envelope. Fancy that, being born in an envelope! When Mum eventually told me all about it, she made me feel very special indeed. One thing adopted children can be absolutely sure of is that they are wanted.

Since becoming an adult I have often thought about what kind of emotions my adoptive parents went through that day – they knew they were going to pick up a baby, so there would be expectation and an element of trepidation, and they would surely be worried about whether they were doing the right thing. What is he going to look like? Why is he up for adoption? Has he got two arms, two legs and a winkle? Especially a winkle – who would choose a son without a Mr Happy?

It must have been very much like going to Battersea Dogs Home, except that there they could have picked the one with the nice face, but here it was the other way round; they were praying that the one with the nice face was the one they were going to get. They probably looked at me and thought they'd been awarded a consolation prize: 'Have we come to the right place or are we at Crufts?'

In those days it was only the perfect specimens who were adopted; the rest were kept in homes and cared for by specialists, quite rightly. I got through the net, however, even though I wasn't perfect. They didn't know about my eyes; you need really good eyes to see through my specs. As I got a bit older you couldn't miss it – I had a lazy eye that pointed everywhere except where it should. So for me it was definitely a lucky draw. I'd spent only three or four months in the children's home and my name must have been pulled out of a hat, because it was very much a raffle as to who was adopted by whom in those days.

I was about seven months old when I began the long journey home to Clayton-le-Moors with the Whittakers, dressed in a bundle of rags. When they got me home they put me on a chair in the parlour and looked at me for a long time. There was little else to do that night, as there was no baby gear in the house, although a pram from three houses down the street had mysteriously turned up in the back garden. So there was Annie at the mill one day, thin as a rake, and the next day pushing me round in a pram – it was 'How to be a Mother in Twelve Hours' by A. Whittaker, with no Angel Gabriel visiting Accrington that year.

'Oh, we didn't know you were having a baby,' said the neighbours. 'Isn't he like his dad!'

Annie smiled a lot but didn't say too much because she didn't know how long she'd be able to keep me. I was a gift on approval, sale or return. Adoption then involved a nine-month period of probation before an adoption hearing to confirm that the circumstances of the natural mother had not changed.

Joe said she should give up her job straight away and he'd be supporting the three of us on his wages of about seven pounds. A surprise was waiting for him when he went in to work the next morning – his kiln at the brickworks had been secretly packed with a pile of baby things brought in by his workmates. The foreman at the brickworks had turned a blind eye to this prank even though it held up the firing of the bricks. Dad didn't mind either, but he had to stay late that night to catch up on his work.

Meanwhile I'm at home on the first day of my trial. I was involved in an audition before I could even speak. I was auditioning to become a proper son and my theatre was the Whittaker household. The lovely thing about it was that the people holding the audition wanted me to get the job. Joe and Annie couldn't change my name until they went back to court at the end of their nine-month probationary period to find out whether or not Ms Williams' position had altered and she had changed her mind. Imagine what was going through Joe and Annie's minds. They could still be asked to hand me back after nine months – I mean, you could get close to a gerbil in that time.

When the day of the final adoption hearing came, Annie and Joe went before the magistrate with me looking bigger and fatter, polished and scrubbed, dressed up fit for a tea party, with my wonky eye still wandering wildly about the courtroom. Ms Williams was asked whether her cir-cumstances had changed and she said that they had not. Then the magistrate said, 'I am now in a position to confirm that Joe and Annie Whittaker may now legally adopt Peter Williams.'

'That sentence lasted three hours,' Annie used to say. She broke down with relief in the courtroom and that was that: I became James Brown Whittaker (Brown was Annie's maiden name) and right there in the courtroom I was rubber-stamped to prove it. Just like the sheep on the Pennines.

2

Sparking Clogs and Rolling Muffins

At eighteen months old I became Joe and Annie's son and heir and they became my legal mum and dad. It was back home to 303 Dill Hall Lane, Church, near Accrington, this time for a definite period of growing up with proper parents.

We had all passed our auditions; I was theirs, legally, irrevocably, for better or worse, for poorer and poorer, in sickliness and in health – the latter proving to be a most significant part of the bargain, as my problem with the wobbly eye was to swivel into insignificance by comparison with a severe bout of diphtheria which I developed a few months later and which left them with a rather scrawny, listless two-year-old. Diphtheria was a killer then and by all accounts I had a rather sickly time as a toddler, punctuated by the chilly stethoscope of the kindly Dr McGovern.

Mum and Dad thought Dr McGovern was the Lady of Lourdes in drag. He was a small and gentle Scot with thick, dark hair plastered back with Brylcreem, which gave off a perfume that clashed with my layer of Vick ointment. My mother was a big believer in Vick and used to rub it on to my chest so liberally that it took my breath away. Mind you, apparently I ought to have been grateful to have been breathing at all.

The worst part about building up my strength was the Friday night equation: two tablespoons liquorice powder

+ one tablespoon water + vigorous stirring = nauseating mixture + unpleasant drink + long Saturday morning.

'This will make you grow big and strong, James,' said Mum.

'Please can I take Beecham's pills instead, like Dad?' I'd beg for an alternative purgative. But Beecham's pills were an adults-only route to regularity. Are they still, I wonder?

The black sticky liquid worked like dynamite. I think Mum believed there was no such thing as natural roughage and had no faith in peristalsis in the human body, so she got out the liquid Dyno-rod every Friday come rain or shine, fruits or vegetables.

Then there were pobbies – lumps of yesterday's bread floating in hot milk and sugar. I ploughed through my morning pobbies, searching for a bit of soggy crust, anything for variety. I never liked them but I had to eat them because if Dad said, 'It's good for you,' I believed him. There on the table, every morning, was this bowl of pobbies, white and steaming, even when I started school. Sometimes I used to nip next door to Mrs Ashton whose house was a pobbie-free zone. Mr Ashton was a believer in fried bread and used to save me a piece, and I really enjoyed my secret early-morning rendezvous with the frying pan at number 305.

My parents didn't have many relatives, so we were more of a contracted family than an extended one. I had a grandad on my dad's side and a grandma on my mum's side (but not for long), the odd uncle and someone called Uncle Billy in Nelson, but that was abroad. Our house in Dill Hall Lane was two up, two down, with a green front door and an outside loo. I did my best to leave my mark along the walls, up the garden path and as far as I could carry my crayon.

We had a good view of the allotments and Enfield Cricket ground was next door. This was the top end of Clayton-le-Moors, the more aspirational side of the canal bridge. The canal was a kind of social dividing line then, separating the have-a-bits towards Accrington and Oswaldtwistle from the have-littles towards Great Harwood, where there were a lot of mills and the laundry and people tended to be poorer.

It's not quite like that now, thank goodness, although I do think there's still very much an awareness of place in heavily industrialized, working-class districts. There's a respect and appreciation of the quirks and different strengths of character fostered in these close communities, still valued even by people who have moved on – certainly by yours truly.

One of my earliest memories is walking to the brickworks with my mum when she took Dad's lunch up to him. She tried to vary the menu, but in 1939 there were liquids and solids – and solids were a bonus. So she used to make soup one day, broth another day. If you found a piece of meat in it you were having stew.

Mum would carry the food up the hill to the works yard in a brown earthenware bowl with a muslin cloth stretched over the top and secured by fine white string. That hill was a long climb to me (although I did the walk recently and it took all of six minutes). As a toddler on a frosty January morning I thought they'd moved a mountain to Accrington just to get lunch to Dad. When I was older I was allowed to carry the bowl on my own. I might have spilled a bit, but by the time I got as far as the brickworks I felt like Edmund Hillary reaching the peak of Everest. And the descent back to base camp held real dangers; my great fear of the quarry on one side of the route was quite rational, because there was a 200-foot drop, guarded by a safety fence made of string that was almost as thin as the sort Mum used to tie up her muslin tops!

When I got back home I used to have a marmalade sandwich and a cup of tea with Mum, who always insisted that I never drank the tea at the same time as eating the sandwich. Much emphasis was placed on chewing food well (so why on earth the Friday-night trial by liquorice-powder?).

I didn't have a lot of toys but I had a treasured tricycle that survived many charges of cowboys and Indians up and down the back lane, where I could swerve behind the garage to hide from the Indians and emerge as Roy Rogers riding

Trigger into the smoky sunset, but only for an hour because he got tired quickly did Trigger.

On summer evenings Dad would take me down to his allotment, which meant that lovely smell of nasturtiums and tomatoes in the greenhouse. I thought Dad's lettuce and tomatoes were the best in the world, and I remember watching him build a cold frame in utter awe and admiration.

When the Second World War broke out I was nearly three years old and Dad was too old to fight. He had served as a medic among the carnage of Ypres and rarely spoke about his experiences of the First World War. There were a few old photographs of him in uniform, kept with his medals in a Barker & Dobson humbug tin in the sideboard. I was allowed to look in the tin and used to break my fingernails trying to open it without help, then I would lay out the medals and straighten the ribbons. Among the photographs were pictures of my mysterious Uncle Jim.

My question, 'What was it like in the war, Daddy?' always elicited a sharp recital of his army number and the same brief story: 'Well, one day I was picked out on parade for having the shiniest boots.' And when pressed Dad would explain that when Kitchener pointed the finger and said 'Your country needs you', he went off with the Accrington boys to do his duty: 'I was one of the first to volunteer in 1914, I went with your Uncle Jim ...' he would say proudly, then quickly and quietly add, 'but he never came back from France.'

Seldom mentioned except in that context, the subject of Uncle Jim was a strangely hallowed grey area. I don't think he was Dad's brother, I just knew that Dad hero-worshipped this 'Uncle Jim', his best pal who had been lost in the war. Although nobody ever told me, I knew that I was named after this 'uncle'.

I didn't grow up with lots of heroic war stories. Not many youngsters did, especially in mid-Lancashire, because probably a large percentage of Accrington's male population had been wiped out in the 1914–18 fracas. What an enormous waste!

In fact, even during the years of the Second World War I don't remember being very much aware that there was a war on. I suppose the Germans didn't think there was very much of value in Accrington, Lancashire. I, however, knew there was. There was Mum and Dad and me and the brickworks, and my little world seemed to remain untouched by the war until the flags were put up for the street parties on VE Day.

One bomb was dropped by accident on a house in Whalley Road, which I remember was left in ruins for years. There was another family friend whom I called Uncle Arthur. He was a Chief Petty Officer on HMS *Vanguard* and used to bring badges home for me. And that's about all the war meant to me. It was only in retrospect, when I grew up – when I was about forty I suppose – that I was able to understand the emotional and economic strife of warfare and realized what pressures and tragedies it had involved for the grown-ups. Talk about being a late developer!

I came through the diphtheria with the help of Dr McGovern and, despite the pobbies and Vick, reached the age of five and went to St James's Infants School in 1942. My first day at school was a big success. I remember walking into the old stone building with Mum and seeing a playroom with big boxes and a sand pit. A sand pit! This was the place for me! When Mum let go of my hand and told me I could go and play in it, I couldn't believe my luck. There were lots of other children to play with and plenty of sand to go round. I didn't have anything like this on Dill Hall Lane.

My first teacher was Miss Pilkington. She had round spectacles, kindly, round features, well-rounded woollen twinsets, and she said, 'Well done, James,' so often that it's not surprising I stayed at the top of the class. Although there was never a lack of support and security at home, my time in Miss Pilkington's class pointed me towards my first real sense of progress and achievement. I was top of the class so I liked

St James's school. Mum had taught me to count and read a few words at home, and when the wonderful Miss Pilkington actually told my mum that I was very bright I believed her.

Fond memories of my early schooldays later made me aware that children need to know how much is thought of them and that adults should remember the importance of giving justified praise. Sadly, those little words of encouragement may not come always naturally to parents who have never been praised themselves as children, so you can get generation after generation of morose under-achievers.

When I became a classroom teacher some twenty years later I would remind myself of 'The Pilkington Principle', remembering how important words of encouragement had been to me in bleak Victorian classrooms. Every child should have a Miss Pilkington; she became the first of my 'Illustriati'. By 'Illustriati' I mean people I admire and who have brightened and enriched my own life by their existence. (There are also the 'Obliterati', fewer in number, who darkened and impoverished my life. Fortunately, they were to cross my path later in life when I was strong enough to compensate for their presence.)

Miss Pilkington never got cross and probably didn't need to, I suppose, because teachers had a good chance of keeping control in the 40s and didn't have parents threatening to break the classroom down.

It was easy to be happy at school when I was top of the class – and a brigadier to boot. The pupils were awarded medals for collecting waste paper and taking it into class. I think I must have stolen a lot, because I became the only brigadier in the school. There were a lot of captains and colonels but only one brigadier and that was me.

The young brigadier who was also top of the class definitely got a touch too perky at times, so Miss Pilkington had to tighten the reins. I remember reciting what must have been an early version of multiplication tables and thinking, 'I'm good at this, so why won't Miss Pilkington let me play the drum?'

But come the music lesson ... 'Please, Miss. Can I have a go on the drum, please?'

'No, James, you take the triangle.'

The triangle! It hardly made a noise befitting the status of a waste-paper brigadier who was top of the class. It probably helped my sense of timing, but I wanted to be a big noise. I used to think, 'Why has Frank got the drum again and I'm stuck with this blessed little tinkling thing?'

Miss Pilkington also put me firmly in my place in the nativity play. I saw myself as one of the three wise men, in grand robes, bearing glittering gold, doing the business. What part did I get? The back end of the donkey.

'But Miss Pilkington, I won't be able to say anything.'

'Exactly, James, the back end of the donkey does not speak,' came the firm reply with, I suspect, a wry smile and a sigh of relief at the prospect of keeping me quiet for a while.

My performance as the back end of the donkey was as boisterous as the back of a donkey can get in a crowded stable. I had studied Dobbin, the milkman's shire horse, and decided not to take him as a model; my donkey was to be an altogether younger, friskier character who unwittingly did a little Fred Astaire dance when the three kings came on stage. Even under cover of a donkey skin made of sacking, my skinny legs wanted to star.

I had made such good friends with Dobbin through my research into method acting that the milkman became known as 'uncle' Joe Bracewell and on Sundays he would let me stand on the cart and hold the reins as a special treat. He was a bald, red-faced, jolly man with a ready smile which exposed his only two teeth. He could have kept a prawn in his mouth for twenty minutes without even bruising it and was renowned for gumming to death a piece of meat, but was nevertheless a very likeable and popular man. I remember his gappy grin, as he used to ladle out the milk for each household from a big urn on his cart.

The morning that Dobbin fell down outside our garden gate was a big tragedy. The faithful old shire horse slipped on the ice, crashed down on his two front knees and couldn't move. There was Joe the milkman, standing in the street with the ladle in his hand and looking down at the collapsed horse between the upended cart shafts, oblivious to the milk streaming from the big urn that had toppled over.

The customers waiting with their jugs gradually took in the scene, then gingerly made their way out into the icy road. About fifteen women and children crowded round to help Joe lift the horse, panting steamy clouds of breath into the frosty air. It was a memorable scene for a young boy; I felt so helpless, with so many people trying and seemingly unable to move Dobbin, but eventually he found his footing and with an enormous effort raised himself back to a standing position one leg at a time.

I was very touched by the sight of the powerful horse struggling to stand up and by Joe Bracewell's sad expression as they clopped away. The day Dobbin fell down was something like having a car crash outside your front door today. Funnily enough, Dobbin now features in my cabaret act as a pseudonym for Mr Happy when he has difficulty in standing to attention. I hereby refute any Freudian connection! Dobbin is as Dobbin does; Mr Happy is as Mr Happy does.

Most of my early memories of schooldays are like a Lowrie painting. During breaks we banged around, sparking our clogs in the playground, with the mill chimneys in the background and the green hills just beyond. I remember the school railings being taken away at the time when any old iron was supposedly put to good use for military purposes. The playground seemed barren without the railings and I was aware of a degree of utility, but had no more carefree times in my short life to compare with the war years. Most of my classmates had big spuds – otherwise known as holes – in their socks, and a lot of them really did have their shirt tails hanging out of the holes in their britches. That was normal; we weren't old enough to make any connection between clogs and spuds and the war.

We weren't in an area that sent off evacuees and we didn't get any sent to us either – they sent evacuees to green farmlands where they had room to breathe, not to places where there were lots of smoking chimneys which made breathing difficult.

Clogs, spuds, rationing and all, growing up around Accrington in wartime didn't seem particularly unpleasant as it was all there was; I suppose you had to be there to appreciate a wartime childhood. There was a sort of grey contentment, but fun doesn't feature very much in my childhood memories. I don't remember ever skipping merrily along to school on a sunny summer's day, and I don't remember those tall, cold classrooms of the dowdy church school with any great affection. The windows were 200-feet high and so near to heaven that the window poles were impossible things to handle, so the air remained still. The smell of carbolic, dusty floors, chalk and the unforgettable aroma of imported school meals remain firmly implanted in my nostalgia bank. Twenty years on I was to spend a lot of time working in similar surroundings. I entered an aromatic time-warp when I began my teaching career in 1959.

There wasn't any joking or teasing at home, yet I was beginning to discover an instinct for performing at school. The rear end of the donkey at St James's engendered in me a desire to entertain, but I would never in a million years have expected my parents to laugh at me. Laughter only seemed to happen when Uncle Arthur occasionally rolled up with some of his friends from the Navy.

One day when I was about seven I was sent down the hill to buy six muffins and the baker handed them to me in a tissue-paper wrapper, knotted at the top. I couldn't handle the package because my hands were too small and the muffins were falling out at all angles on to the pavement. The easiest way to transport them home appeared obvious: I could hold two and roll the other four. Watching the white rounds of bread wobbling up the hill made me giggle with glee. I must have thought that no one would notice the damage when I got back home.

I don't think Mum had ever seen muffins with tyres on them before, and her expression told me that I had fallen seriously short of making the grade as a muffin deliverer. I was sent to bed in disgrace with not so much as a grubby muffin to eat for supper, but I'd rather like to think that Mum and Dad had a little chuckle about it afterwards. They didn't have to tell me that they didn't want a precocious little show-off on their hands, for I knew full well that honesty and hard work were the main objectives of the Whittaker household.

I also knew, from a very early age, that I was expected to get a white-collar job. It was an unspoken promise that I should not follow my father into the brickworks, that I was fortunate enough to be able to do better than he had and indeed owed it to him to carry on his process of moving ever onwards and upwards in the world.

Dad told everyone else how well I was doing and he obviously thought the world of me, but he never told me. I had to hang on to the words of Miss Pilkington for many years; if a teacher said I was bright, I couldn't be completely stupid.

I was very much aware that my father worked hard. Many times when Mum and I had walked up to the brickworks to take him his soup in the basin at dinner time, I had watched him eat it amazingly quickly because, as a skilled setter, he had to hurry back to work to keep ahead of the fire.

The brickworks was a dusty, mucky, sweaty place. Today's Friends of the Earth folk would go there to commit hara-kiri. Dad explained to me that Nori bricks were so called because they were so hard and the name spelled iron backwards. He would come home late from work sometimes and tell me he'd had to supervise a special assignment of bricks being loaded on to railway wagons for a long trip to the Far East to build kilns and oil containers. I was very impressed because I knew that the Far East was a lot farther away than Blackpool.

I was proud of the bricks he made and I thought Dad deserved his extra two tomatoes from the allotment on Sundays.

3

Blackpool, the World Beyond

Blackpool has a lot to answer for in the early chapters of my life. We started going there every year for one week of the Accrington holiday Wakes after the war ended and Dad got a new job at the dyeworks. No brochures or travel agents were necessary; there was absolutely no question of going anywhere else.

Jumping off the train at Blackpool North, I would stand and inhale the holiday aroma of the steam from the trains blending with the slightly musty leather smell of our suitcases on their one and only annual outing, and the heady fragrance that is forever Blackpool – the marriage of a bracing topnote of ozone with a strong and reliable base of haddock and chips. It still hasn't changed, except for a hint of *eau de* McDonalds that was to come later.

From the station we'd walk to the North Bank Private Hotel via Talbot Road, where there was always the thrill of seeing the sea for the first time as the North Pier and promenade swept into view. The hotel was about half a mile north along the promenade. It was my idea of heaven at £7 a week (full board for an adult): right next to the sea and with a good view of the straw-hatted toffs who stayed at the Imperial Hotel next door. We'd quickly unpack and spend Saturday afternoon finding out what shows were on, choosing three and booking the best seats we could afford.

I climbed up the wall with Yana the singer full of eastern promise, marvelled at the exotic Winifred Atwell at the piano, picked many a chicken with the South African songstress Eve Boswell, sat spellbound by the great juggler Rudy Cardenas and heard all the old ones, new ones, loved ones, neglected ones of Semprini, who played and behaved like a very shy, unassuming man. Semprini had formerly worked as pianist with big bands, then came an opening in variety for a good solo piano player and he was pushed into it between Charlie Kunz and Russ Conway.

'Can you hear me Mother?' bawled Sandy Powell, one of the funniest ventriloquists the world has known, whose lips moved more than his dummy's – how clever, to create so much laughter from skilled ineptitude. But how naive we must have been in the 50s actually to listen to a ventriloquist on the radio! Jimmy Jewel and Ben Warris's hilarious comedy routines were also classics, as was Frank Randle's outrageous hiking outfit; George Formby cleaning his windows; Betty Driver singing her songs before she pulled her pints at the Rovers Return; Bill Waddington as Witty Willy from Lancashire, a comic before he became a lodger on 'Coronation Street'. I remember the magic of Gracie Fields' *Sally*; Michael Holliday's *Some Day I'm Going To Write*, and Joseph Locke, singing his *Goodbye* every night and never tiring of returning. Norman Evans spoke to us over the garden wall and we laughed along with Albert Modley's 'I'ntit Grand When Yer Daft!' and Rob Wilton in his fireman sketch, pleading with a woman on the telephone to keep the fire going until the engine could get there.

The best timer of a line in the business was Jimmy James who created that hilarious tripartite lunatic asylum with his friends Eli Woods and Roy Castle. There was Freddie Frinton, the best teetotal 'drunk' to stumble the boards, Morecambe and Wise, Mike and Bernie Winters, Al Read, Ted Lune, Nat Jackley, the best funny-walking guardsman in the world ... and many more. At legendary Blackpool theatres – the Opera House, Hippodrome, North Pier, Central Pier, South Pier, Winter Gardens, Feldman's, later to become the Queen's – I saw some of the biggest names in Britain. And some of the smallest bodies: Jimmy Clitheroe appeared there quite a lot!

We'd go to the first house of each show (in the 40s I was too young to go to the second) and afterwards we walked to Beth's Café down at Gynn Square for a fish and chip supper. What joy! I know it's been said a thousand times by a thousand people, but they really were the best fish and chips in the world.

I've always liked the water, but prefer to be on it rather than in it, so my Woolworth's cossie never got wet enough to hang round my knees. Those maroon knitted swimming trunks in the cold sea came well down on the list of thrills after the shows, the pleasure beach and the motor boats on the marina at Bispham.

Another annual feature of Blackpool was a trip to Fleetwood, where the trams actually run on sleepers and are fenced off, so you felt you were going on a long train journey. It's true that some old lady would always ask the conductor, 'Will I get an electric shock if I put my foot on the track?'

'Only if you get your other leg on the overhead wire,' came the traditional reply.

Blackpool was our Disneyworld, the greatest show on earth. And, truth to tell, it still is. There was simply nowhere else to go on holiday. There were 'Skegness Is So Bracing' posters on the railway station but no one ever thought of going there; it was a foreign land, outside our world. The Tower, the shows, the prom ... this was Fantasia. Blackpool even had superior brickwork – Dad used to point out the copings and decorative work, the beautifully moulded caps on gate pillars and the hemispherical caps on brick walls and say proudly, 'Look, those are all Nori bricks.' I firmly believed that my father had made every brick in Blackpool with his own hands.

All this was a long, long way away from the tall cold

classrooms of Accrington and the mountainous walk to deliver Dad's lunch.

At my junior school, All Saints C of E Primary School, Clayton-le-Moors, I was delighted to find another Miss Pilkington, sister of the first and illustrious Miss P. in the infants school. While I never made it into her class, the Pilkington Principle prevailed at All Saints, even though I was faced with much greater competition. The headmaster was Jimmy Baldwin, who was a wonderful bulldog – strict in manner, severe in appearance, with an appealing resemblance to Jimmy James. There was a twinkle in his eye that showed his strictness was tempered with warmth and understanding. He was a fine teacher in the way that Bernard Manning is such a skilful comic – naked viciousness toned down with a lot of affection and cleverly concealed kindness. I had great respect for Jimmy Baldwin. And I was frightened to death of him.

All Saints school was black. It was surrounded by cotton mills and a dyeworks. Huncoat pit and power stations were quite close by and, depending on which way the wind blew, you got soot or sulphur.

Dinnertimes fascinated me for the first few weeks at my new school. The food came in cylindrical metal containers with lids on. They were supposed to be insulated, but they weren't and they always seemed to contain the same food – cold cabbage. Pudding was rice pudding or rice pudding with a speck of jam in it so you could mix it all together and pretend it was something else. I never liked milk (the pobbies had done me in) so rice pudding was no thrill, and I used to give away my milk in the compulsory milk breaks.

The teacher who now kept me on my toes with my multiplication tables was Ben Ramsden. Today he would be jailed. In those days he was hero-worshipped because we learned our times tables in his class and he used little gimmicks to help us learn, such as hitting pupils around the head with a long ruler if they made a mistake. In his class I even got confident with the chanting of the tricky seven times tables, but I was facing more serious competition at junior school than I had done in the infants. My class position plummeted to seventh place in a class of forty-five, and I couldn't avoid breaking the bad news at home. Mum was devastated and Dad took the matter with grave seriousness: 'There has to be a reason for this,' he said. 'I want to know why you came seventh and I want to know now.'

'Because there's six better than me,' I answered and remember realizing that this hurt him more than a bit. Joe and Annie had got me as a sale item and wanted me to turn out a collector's piece. I wasn't resentful about their attitude because I was just as disappointed as they were.

The biggest crisis of my primary school days happened when I got into a fight with the 'cock' of the School over a football. I knew as soon as I confronted Frank Davis that I was in for trouble. In the scuffle that followed I put my elbow through a classroom window. I was mortified, I felt instantly transformed into a vandal of the lowest order. A custodial sentence seemed not to be out of the question, so prison loomed and, worse than that, I had to face Dad when he got home from work. My whole world collapsed at the end of the day when, in a state of extreme panic, I had to stand with Jim Baldwin at the school gates to meet Mum.

The broken window was a very small one and wouldn't have cost much to replace, as labour was about fourpence a month. It wasn't the damage I'd done that made me panic but the act of vandalism, the fact that I had actually broken a window.

Fortunately the whole episode was put to rest in a few minutes. 'Mrs Whittaker, James has been in a bit of trouble. He's had a fight.' Jimmy Baldwin began in his grave tones. 'But we have dealt with the problem and he doesn't usually break windows, so please don't worry about it. He's a good lad.' I know that the headmaster must have sensed my remorse and also my eternal gratitude for his words to my Mum.

Joe and Annie's son did not break windows. As a youngster

I was getting all those messages about right and wrong – 'Don't ever lie, don't ever cheat.' I was starting to learn that society would crumble without these ground rules. Dad always worked towards getting out of the brickworks and to improve our lot in life, and he inspired me, by quiet example, always to aim to do better things. He was a man of great, wordless integrity. I remember that just after we sold the house in Dill Hall Lane in 1944 to move to a detached bungalow, a man came to the door and offered my dad £50 more for the house than the price he'd accepted. Now fifty quid was a lot of money during the war but Dad wouldn't do it. He'd made an agreement and he wouldn't break his word.

It's true to say that I was becoming a bit of a performer in the classroom, but the idea that little boys become showmen to avoid being bullied has been done to death. Yes, I was bullied a bit and teased for being thin, for the wandering eye, for wearing glasses, and I used to get out of it by trying to be Jack the Lad. I was a bubbly character who didn't make much of an impression on the football pitch and would rather go to the cinema alone on Monday nights than play out in the streets, but that didn't put me on a direct route to showbusiness. The big challenge was getting school reports that satisfied my father and trying to get a surplice out of the Reverend Kenneth Houghton.

My mother wanted me to be in the choir. I couldn't sing well but that didn't deter Mum at all. Sunday night always meant walking with Mum to Evensong at All Saints Parish Church and leaving her at the church gate to nip round the back, over the slippery leaves and into a musty back room to don my cassock, which is what a probationary choir member got to wear to walk behind the choir procession. You had to serve your time before you got a surplice and in my case it seemed as though I had sung my way through a million Sunday evenings and a million Tuesday night choir practices without being properly acknowledged. I didn't want to be there, but it seemed to be an unavoidable weekly duty, so if I had to be there I wanted the proper gear, I wanted to be in the choir as opposed to walking behind it; I wanted to wear the proper team strip and not some baggy, drab old cassock.

I began to think that the Reverend Kenneth Houghton disliked me. I'd try to catch his eye when he came to take the school assemblies, so that he could see for himself my great and overpowering need for a surplice. But I never got one and that is one of my earliest memories of the feeling of coming second, not thinking myself quite good enough. Ken Houghton probably knew how important his choir was to my mother but, as he was later to try to impress upon me, 'God moves in a mysterious way.' He certainly moved in a mysterious way in my childhood because Sundays were the most miserable day of my week, a bleak and tedious ritual of boring Sunday School and cassock-draped evenings. Even the hymn *Lead Us Heavenly Father Lead Us* seemed to have no end.

The only happy memories I have of that church are the times my mother took me round the cemetery at the top of Dill Hall Lane, along the paths between the graves, to learn to ride my first proper bicycle. I gave up and went home nursing my bruises many times before I got the knack, but patience was Mum's virtue. That's what she was best at – gentle perseverance and quiet industry. I wish she could have come for a drive with me in my first Bentley, but that wasn't to be. As it was, she was happy to see me ride my first bicycle.

I can understand why more people might commit suicide between five and seven o'clock on Sunday evenings in Britain than at any other time in the week. My own children were certainly never compelled to go to church, because my memories of religion are all about formality and sitting quiet for a long time not understanding what anyone was saying.

Kenneth Houghton (The Rev.) was a social rather than religious icon; such was his standing in our community of mill workers that I can even remember his car – he had an

Austin Seven with the registration number PRM 241, I think.

Registration numbers always seem to etch themselves on my memory. The first van we ever had was RTC 786, I believe, and I remember Uncle Dick's registration number was BTC 284, definitely. I used to come home from school at All Saints and run to the bottom of Dill Hall Lane to look for his car parked outside our house, because if it was there I knew I could go and sit in it and pretend to drive it. Uncle Dick wouldn't mind. He was always good fun.

Henry Gilbraith's vehicles also fascinated me. My walk to school took me past Gilbraith's garage. Now there was a man I admired. When he bought his first two trucks I was very impressed with the stylish way he had his name painted in big gold letters on the side. I charted his progress by the number of lorries in the yard and eventually counted a gleaming line of twenty-three. Nowadays when I see his tankers on the motorway I still remember his bold gold beginnings at the garage on Whalley Road, not far from the bomb site; from wreckage to success in just 200 yards.

When the 11-plus loomed, I saw it as a step on the road to my dream of owning a car of my own. The exam was a massive watershed in those days, but a few months before I was due to take it I had to change schools to Percy Street Junior School in Nelson, because we moved house to a greengrocer's shop at 158 Railway Street, Nelson. Dad had been made a foreman at the brickworks and was able to set up a small greengrocer's business. My position in class plummeted to twentieth at Percy Street and the more my mathematics fell out of bed along with my position in class, the more I fretted about the possibility of failing the 11-plus.

However, there was a big high spot in that year, which I will never forget. Good old Uncle Dick – who still had his Morris 8, registration number BTC 284 (definitely), but now resided in Market Street, Bury, Lancs – gave me the present of my life. I remember the occasion vividly. Everything was still in short supply after the war. Sweets, clothing, even some foods, certainly meat and bananas, were hard to get. A leather football was completely out of the question. Uncle Dick made me stand facing the wall in the corner of the parlour of his council house in Bury. I was instructed to close my eyes and I distinctly remember hearing the sound of a ball bouncing on the linoleum floor. I could hardly believe my ears – surely not a football? For me? Even a primary school only had one between six classes, and that was 250 children.

'Turn round and open your eyes,' commanded Uncle Dick. This I did, and my ears had not deceived me. There in Uncle Dick's hands was a size four, rich brown leather football with a neat cream lace. I was almost speechless with delight but still managed to say 'Thank you'. I remember I clutched that ball to my chest for the whole of the day, including the journey home on the bus. Mum told me many times afterwards how she tried to take the ball from me whilst I was asleep, but I held it in a vice-like grip. In 1947 a football was not to be parted with lightly.

I took the ball to school the next day and when we played with it I felt personally scuffed every time the ball was kicked. Of all the possessions I've ever had, of all the many thoughtful gifts I've received, of all the many presents I've bought for myself, that football remains the most memorable. Don't talk to me about keeping your feet on the ground!

When the letter containing my 11-plus exam results arrived at home, Mum opened it very carefully and read it in her usual hesitant manner, nervous of any type of official letter. It was the brown envelope syndrome. The authorities favoured the contorted approach to letter-writing in an attempt to evince respect. Words like 'pass' or 'fail' would have been too obvious.

'Er, I think you've passed. It says "... your examination results have entitled you to be considered for a place at Nelson Grammar School", but it just says you've been *considered* for a place at the Grammar school. You'd better nip down to

Barry's on Carlton Street – his mother's expecting him to go to the grammar school. You can compare the letter with his.'

I soon came running back. 'Yes, Mum, I've passed! Barry's got the same letter as me. It says "considered" as well, and he's definitely going to the grammar school. His mum said so.'

'That's good news,' said Mum. 'Well done, you're a clever lad. We'll have to sort out your uniform next.'

I ran down the road in my clogs, waving the letter, to meet my father as he arrived home from work.

'Dad, Dad . . . I've passed!'

'Well done,' he murmured and just patted me on the head and walked on.

I'm sure I've made my own mistakes with my children – most parents do – but that moment upset me so much I will never forget it. I was gutted. There was no excitement, no enthusiasm on the part of my Dad, I didn't get anything like the big reaction I'd hoped for.

What I did get was a green grammar school blazer with a grammar school badge, the symbol of achievement that Mum declared too good to wear for school! As the youngest pupil in the district ever to have passed the 11-plus, I was noticeably the youngest first former at Nelson Grammar School. Having an August birthday gave me some flexibility in the education system, but being a mere ten-year-old with some brains, dodgy eyesight and scrawny stature offered little hope of disguising the fact that I was, for a year or so at least, destined to be the little tiddler of the whole school. My first two weeks of term were spent treading water. I was the new boy, the youngest in the school, and everybody wanted to test me until they eventually realized I was not much of a challenge to any of my classmates.

A child's life in Lancashire in the post-war years didn't engender great ambitions; survival was the first post. I headed towards my teens aware of a lot of empty space between my ears. With bananas still on ration, the height of my aspirations was a Mars bar every two weeks, to be eaten at two sittings, although I do remember one glorious day when I got my hands on a whole box of fruit pastilles and I ate the whole lot behind the toffee shop just south of Nelson Grammar School.

4

Green Greengrocer's Son

My NHS glasses and the legs from a sparrow-transplant blocked any hope of a heated rush into puberty. In a quietly independent sort of way I almost sank to oblivion in my first years at grammar school, but I used any innate wit and guile I could call upon to just about stay afloat.

I went through a phase of desperately wanting a brother and asked one of my friends at school if he would consider the role. I had never quite worked out why all my friends had brothers and sisters and I didn't, so I was relieved when it was all made clear to me with the story of my adoption.

In my first year at grammar school my mother found a perfect moment to explain. 'Adopted Child Saves Dog From Canal' ran the front-page headline in the *Nelson Leader* I was reading over my bubble and squeak one Monday lunchtime.

'Mum, what does "adopted" mean?' I asked.

'It means that when a baby is born and his mother can't afford to keep him, he stays in a children's home for a few weeks until his new parents can come to pick him up. You're adopted, you know. That's how me and Dad got you, from a children's home in Liverpool.'

She seemed very relaxed about it, but years later she told me that she and Dad had agonized over when and how to tell me, and what my reaction was going to be. In fact it was very ingeniously done – just putting the newspaper where I couldn't miss seeing the heading, then explaining very briefly because I had to get back to school in the afternoon.

'So if you hadn't taken me I might have stayed in the children's home?' I mused.

'I suppose you might have, yes,' said Mum.

I remember feeling quite excited about it and thinking, 'Oh, well done, Mum!' as I rushed off back to school to tell my friends.

'Eh, guess what?' I shouted as we banged a football around the playground. 'I'm *adopted*! I've got *two* mums!'

When I got home after school I wanted to know more. The washing was all put away, the house was calmer, so I sat in the front room with Mum for half an hour while she told me the story of my adoption in the way I've tried to recapture earlier in this book, in a way that made me feel special.

Some of the details were quite distressing for Annie. I particularly remember her being shocked and upset by the harsh way the magistrate had spoken to Ms Williams at the adoption hearing. In those days her actions were seen as unquestionably sinful and the magistrate treated this poor unmarried mother like a leper. Annie said she had felt such a deep sorrow for the mother who gave me away that she had never forgotten, and I suppose she thought I should know about that.

If Ms Williams is still alive and knows that I am her son, I hope she is in good health and takes pleasure in reading this book. I do hope her fortunes improved after 1937. But I've never understood why some adopted children decide to seek out their natural parents when they reach adulthood. It seems to me most ungracious and ungrateful behaviour. The only reason an adopted child need know his natural roots might be to establish any special medical history.

Of course, I wondered about my 1937 parents sometimes. Although my father never talked about the adoption business – I can see that would have been asking too much from a man for whom actions spoke so much louder than words – I was able to indulge in a little light-hearted speculation with Mum.

'I could be the son of a ship's captain, I could be a million-aire ... or the heir to the throne ...'

'Oh, yes?' Mum would smile because she knew I was content with the life I had. 'So do you want to go and find out?'

'No, I'll have another plate of chips and stay here. And besides, it's raining outside.'

Having seen my own children grow up, those moments now mean so much more to me, because I realize how Mum and Dad must have felt, what hopes they had for me – and how I was about to shatter most of them for a while by sliding into the doldrums of academia at grammar school.

I was fairly adept at drawing and printing, so for a while I nurtured a dream of the adult Jim sitting on a stool and drawing at a leisurely pace, as a draughtsman or an architect. This image seemed to be in line with Mum and Dad's hopes for me in a collar-and-tie career, but the idea evaporated into the industrial mists of Nelson even before my first dismal school report.

Suddenly I was not an achiever. The Nelson Grammar School blazer with its gold leaf badge, a symbol of achievement in those days, was kept in pristine condition in the wardrobe. It was supposed to be a school uniform but I was only allowed to wear it on Sundays for church, where it compensated but partially for my never having attained the level of surplice-wearer in that confounded choir.

All the excitement of passing the 11-plus ebbed away as I realized at a bewildering speed that I was making no impression in the classroom, in the playground or on the sportsfield.

Bleak school reports didn't get much response at home. The words 'could do better' started to appear and must have disappointed my parents as much as they disappoint me now when I see them applied to another person. My heart would sink as I waited for my father to open and read my school reports, but if my parents felt angry or let down they must have known how to handle it because there were no threats or angry scenes, just as there had been no promises or scenes of celebration when I'd been the little star with the Misses Pilkington.

By now Dad had moved to a job at Jopson Bardsley & Jopson, a dyeworks in Nelson. Instead of coming home with a thick coating of red brick dust to remove from his person he was now a dust-free zone with just the odd tint and a slight chemical smell which were easy to wash away. He was no longer a foreman, but that didn't bother him because he had bought a greengrocer's shop, determined to become self-sufficient in stages. Aspirations were never spoken of; they were part of the fabric of life.

We lived behind and over the shop and Mum applied a lot of hard work and personality to running it. I'd set off to walk the two miles to school just before eight in the morning and come home at four to get on with my homework. Or, if I was very lucky, I escaped to help price up some potatoes or bag up a few tomatoes. On the odd occasion, and under close supervision, I was allowed to serve a customer.

Following Dad's ablutions, conversation at the tea table was always minimal. Mealtimes were not a focal point for family discussions – because of the shop, meals were staggered, and often interrupted by the bell on the shop door. It was protocol not to display feelings; Mum was Queen, Dad was King, infallible in my eyes, and I was trainee king. Looking back I think that my poor performance at Nelson Grammar was affecting my relationship with my father. I knew I wasn't the success story he had hoped for and strands of disappointment were already weaving between us.

We'd come a long way from the two grades of soup on offer in Clayton-le-Moors. We weren't affluent but we were solvent and I'd say we probably had three figures in the bank by then. To be £3.10s in the black was a great achievement two years after the war, so the stew was now more solid, with easily identifiable pieces of meat in it.

Some evenings I was allowed to rearrange the chrome shelf fitting in the window, which was the highlight of the shop. Two hexagonal chrome rings supported two glass shelves, with the whole thing suspended on chains hanging from hooks in the ceiling. Mum was very pleased with this acquisition and took great pride in changing the display every week. After a few weeks of rearranging the shelf with the limited stock available the novelty wore off for me, but I took a renewed personal interest in the display when toffees came off ration. Riley's Chocolate Toffee Rolls, Nutall's Mintoes and Barker & Dobson's humbugs were in great demand and tasted best when I did a quick stock-take and lost a couple temporarily until they later appeared in my trouser pocket. A scoop of eight toffees sent the pointer on the Avery scales over the two-ounce mark, which meant I could feel justified in saving one for myself if I was selling a particularly heavy quarter of a pound to a fat person. The sprinkling of guilt made toffees all the more enjoyable as I tucked into them in the back room, listening to the Bush radio – a huge mahogany monument with cream plastic buttons. Many an index finger has been severely bruised whilst pressing the stiff buttons in an attempt to find the Home Service.

I was a regular listener to Ted Ray's comedy show 'Ray's A Laugh' and to Peter Brough the ventriloquist. I'm still convinced that Peter Brough didn't move his lips on radio and that his dummy Archie Andrews once said 'gollocks'. Another favourite was at ten past one in the afternoon on Saturdays – Cyril Stapleton's Showband Show featured Bert Weedon on guitar and Alfred Marks as compère.

Directly across from our greengrocer's shop was Eddie Gray, who ran one of those 'sliced-things' shops that predated the delicatessen, selling cold meats, potted meats and other chilled goods that kept his hands permanently red. His 'Good morning, Jim' was also a rather cold commodity for someone who lived only a few yards away, but I suppose Whittaker's greengrocer's was the competition. He sold delicious ice-cream that he made himself with his big red hands in the back of the shop. You'd watch him push it into the cone with the scoop and hope that he was pushing really hard so that he could squash in an extra dollop. I'm sure he sold me short sometimes, because when I got to the bottom of my cone it was often empty.

Another high point of life in Railway Street was our first washing machine. It was cream, with an electric mangle and a fearsome agitator contraption, and it was called the Fisher Automatic – which would certainly contravene the Trade Descriptions Act today, as it was noisy, inefficient and needed a lot of help.

Coming home from school for lunch on Mondays always promised the welcoming aroma of bleach and bubble and squeak – a memorable combination – and the arrival of the Fisher machine added wrap-around sound effects. 'Keep out of the kitchen, the washer's on!' was a common warning from Mum.

At the beginning of the wash the machine was standing in the corner on the uneven flagstones and by the end it had danced its way so far across the kitchen that it came to share our dinner with us at the table. The machine had the ability to ride the joints between the flagstones and seemed to enjoy working over variations in levels offered by the raffia mat. Until she learned to trust the Fisher, Mum would lift out all the washing when the washer stopped and drop it into a tub for another beating with the copper posser (which I'll define for the new-tech generation as an inverted colander attached to the end of a pole, used as a plunger to pound viciously several garments immersed in soapy water). The electric mangle was approached with an action similar to Arkwright getting the change out of his till in the 'Open All Hours' TV series. Ronnie Barker would have been proud of Mum's agility as she gingerly engaged the mangle and then leapt back a few yards to watch and worry.

I'm not sure whether the nervous energy expended justified

an almost dry and heavily wrinkled shirt with buttons broken by the mangle, but the technological age was upon us and, after the Fisher, the quiet workings of a car engine held no fear for me.

My first 'vehicle' was a two-wheel miniature handcart that I was allowed to use to deliver to the more important customers on Friday nights. One evening I painted 'Whittakers' Greengrocer's' on the side in white emulsion and rattled off down the street full of pride at my promotional handiwork and fondly remembering the time I'd seen Henry Gilbraith's first truck with his name neatly painted in gold. I imagined myself with a whole fleet of grocery carts, then vans, then tankers like Mr Gilbraith's, but then it started to rain and daydreaming no longer worked as an anaesthetic. The rain washed away the painted sign into white zebra stripes and with it my fleeting career prospects in signwriting, retailing or haulage. The customers were as miserable as ever. I was very happy to park my cart and get back home to the *Dandy* and *Beano*.

I was a prolific reader of comics, which didn't accelerate my academic progress. At twenty-third in the class, which I was, it helped to be good at sport, which I wasn't. I might have been a fair soccer player but I wore glasses, the sign of frailty that no team wanted; you either had to take off spectacles to play or keep them on and prepare for the crash.

Footballs of the day weighed three hundredweight when wet and were laced up with cable wire. You'd pray that an oncoming header would make contact when the lace was facing away from your forehead. Consequently, I wasn't at all keen on serious soccer and perfected my role of staying close to the edge of the pitch at all times. On the few occasions that I was passed the ball, I discovered that I could run quite fast. Then someone realized that I had a slow heartbeat, so from then on I was a runner.

Running became my saving grace at school. With running there wasn't a teamful of competitive hormones to contend with and, best of all, I could do it without touching anybody or getting my glasses broken. Although I had lost my sickly appearance and was in good physical shape in adolescence, I was in bad shape up top – the will to succeed escaped me. I registered my first clear feeling of insecurity when I was entered for the 880 yards (athletics hadn't yet gone decimal) in the second year inter-house sports at Nelson Grammar. I was winning the race for Thursby house, almost at the finishing tape, when I remember my pal Barry Whitham shouting, 'Come on, Jim, you can win!'

I panicked because I hadn't been a winner since St James's Infant School. That second-best feeling took over and I thought, 'I can't do this.' I should have romped home, but I slowed down and gave away the first place to a guy called Sidebottom. Fancy giving first place to someone called Sidebottom – even his name didn't imply forward motion! He actually went on to become a first-class athlete.

The PE master was the enigmatic George Robey. I never understood whether he was devious, very strict or just two-faced. I once played football in a form match and scored thirteen goals and when Robey asked me how I thought I'd done it, I said, 'I was in the right place at the right time.' And Robey said this was the sign of a great soccer player, so I felt encouraged. He even mentioned the fact to the House Captain – I think his name was Cook – but I was never in his tour brochure, not even as a bargain offer when it came to picking reserves.

My classroom performance didn't improve at Nelson Grammar and I took my abysmal standard of work to Accrington Grammar in the third form, when Mum and Dad bought a busier shop on Green Lane in Padiham. He left the dyeworks to run the shop with Mum because this business could sustain all of us. It was a newsagent's/grocer's/greengrocer's/general store and off-licence. In fact this shop sold most things; on a good day you could get a gear box for a 1937 Morris 8, oil extra, bottom shelf, left-hand side.

Allowed to venture out alone to explore the wilds of Padiham

I stumbled upon the First Padiham St Leonard's Boy Scouts Group and was lured into the pack with the promise of bugle lessons. Wearing neckerchief and woggle atop a khaki scout shirt and shorts that emphasized my weaknesses, I quickly rose to the position of chief bugler in the band and got badges for tying knots, lighting fires, translating from English to French and back, and other skills that took no time at all to master. I loved the Scouts; I was an academic there.

St Leonard's Scout Group gave a grammar school boy the chance to be a big fish in a little pond. All my peers in the troop had a real sense of values. Not for them books, numbers, homework and correct spellings – oh no, a Woodbine, plots and schemes to upend the neighbourhood harmlessly and wild adventures in the woods behind Gawthorpe Hall, which included firelighting and hiding behind bushes. I have to emphasize that the firelighting was not an attempt at arson but simply lighting little twigs to get that friendly fireside singsong and maybe roast the odd potato. I could win in this theatre.

Most of my spare time and energy became dedicated to scouts and bugling. I suppose I was a clown at school, too timid to be really naughty, and a bit of a loner at home. I do remember looking forward to going to the cinema on my own as soon as I was old enough, buying a bag of chips, coming home and going to bed without talking to anyone. I wasn't consciously lonely, but I had few friends and growing up never seemed easy, let alone enjoyable.

It was while we were in the shop at Padiham that we acquired our first pet, a delightful King Charles spaniel called Bess. She used to accompany me occasionally on my paper round, though very seldom lasted the whole course before turning back for home. I could do my morning and evening paper rounds in fourteen minutes wearing my sandals that were best for running and I think that helped me with my cross-country.

Work and newspapers featured heavily in my life as a

newsagent's son, but no one, least of all me, saw me as a boy who would grow up to feature in the newspapers himself.

My move to Accrington Grammar in the third year wasn't easy, but I had made my new friends in the scout troop. Mum was very pleased that I was at this particular school because her own mother had started a school meals system there, so she felt there was a family connection.

I made few ties, either with the classroom teachers or the frightening headmaster Ben Johnson, who wore a permanently worried look and commanded great respect. During assemblies, he could strike terror in the heart of every pupil in the school with a slight movement of his chin and a pursing of his mouth over tobacco-stained teeth. When he was truly angry Ben Johnson's dark eyes seemed to glitter with menace from behind his sedate horn-rimmed glasses.

I always sought Dad's approval but didn't expect much. He worked long hours, so I couldn't be disappointed if he didn't spend much time with me. Going to football matches with him was an honour, and Saturday mornings would be full of anticipation if I knew we were going to watch Blackburn Rovers. Dad would lace up his Saxone shoes in the dining room, fold the yellow scarf tightly across his neck and put on his beige mac. I would copy his every action. I honestly believed that Saxone shoes were the best in the world because Dad wore them and when I was eventually allowed to wear long trousers at fourteen they had to be grey flannel, exactly like his.

If Dad said that the best place to watch a football match was near the half-way line in the enclosure, then it was. It never occurred to me that it cost four bob in the stands. We would meet up with a few regulars in the crowd – Charlie from Great Harwood, Harry from Rishton and John with the checked cap – and the fact that most of my contributions to the conversation were ignored didn't deter me. As we made our way back home, my mood would mirror Dad's; if Blackburn Rovers lost I was disappointed for him, not for the team.

★

While high marks and glowing reports still escaped me, my athletics went from strength to strength at Accrington Grammar. I ran for the school, even if it was because no one else wanted to do it. Luckily, there was also Fred Hartley – an impressive gourmet-shaped PE teacher who did a lot of his training in the kitchen. He was very keen on the character-forming rigours of cross-country and didn't pester me to get into team games as long as I persevered with my running.

One of my claims to athletic fame is that I captained the school team that included Ron Hill, who went on to be one of our greatest Olympic marathon runners. Whereas I wasn't above a few secret Woodbines before a run, Ron's dedication to his own physique set him apart from the rest. He ran for the world every day.

My swift progress with the bugle in the scout band prompted me to ask Mum and Dad to buy me a trumpet, which they duly did. I suppose any sign of initiative or positive growth in any direction gave them hope for me!

My Selmer Invicta trumpet opened up the world of Dixieland jazz. In the fourth form I was allowed to take my trumpet into school because we had managed to form a band which even had one of the teachers in it – an English teacher called Ian Holworth. As he allowed band members to call him Ian, he was considered very progressive in the 50s and was frowned upon by the non-jazzy staff at the school. We'd go to Les Whitemoss's house and play Jimmy Lally arrangements rearranged to reflect our ability.

I'd been fiddling about with my trumpet for a while by this time, but never bothered to learn to read music. I thought I could get away with it. When the lads said, 'Right, play a solo Jim,' I'd stand up and press any old valve. It was horrendous. I don't know how they put up with it. I must have had something going for me that I wasn't aware of. Perhaps I was a motivator, a communicator, a little asset or an interesting liability. For some unmusical reason I was drifting into the performing arts. Of course, we weren't good enough to play in public, we weren't even good enough to play outside the front room and, sad to relate, the unofficial jazz band of Accrington Grammar didn't have one groupie.

Looking back on those days I wish upon wish that I had applied more discipline to my trumpet playing. I bitterly regret not having learned to master the instrument and my limited repertoire is now one of my biggest frustrations.

5

Church, Trumpet and Crumpet

Girls never featured much in my teens, although I know that may be hard to imagine today. The grammar school was an all-boys establishment but at least I was part of the in-crowd at home, which meant I could look forward to two hours of old-time dancing every Saturday night at Padiham's fleshpot, St Leonard's Parish Church Hall. In this den of adolescent passion and vice we strutted our stuff to the throbbing melodies of the veleta, the military two-step and, yes, even the Gay Gordons (in the 1950s this meant a happy dancing Scotsman). This was our chance to be rebellious. We were ruffians, we were tearaways, sometimes we didn't even bother to salute during the military two-step. And this was where I first noticed that girls had lumps.

Every week I'd walk into that church dance swinging my trumpet in a linen bag with a drawstring that my mother had specially tailored for the instrument. I sometimes wonder why she chose material of such limited protective quality. I may have noticed a few heads falling into hands in anticipation of the noise to come from the contents of the bag, but I was undeterred. In the interval I used to play *Oh Mein Papa* – every week, same time, same place, same tune. Only once did I try *Cherry Pink*, later to become part of my repertoire of three tunes, in front of the Padiham audience. I forgot the tune and reverted to *Oh Mein Papa*

41

after a few bars.

Nobody ever asked me to play, but I stood up and opened
the linen bag anyway. The St Leonard's fleshpotters couldn't
dance to it easily; they couldn't even listen to it in comfort,
but I'd paid my one shilling and sixpence and they were going
to get my money's worth.

I did have some local inspiration for this blatant show-
manship, as Eddie Calvert, who had put *Oh Mein Papa* at
number one in the popular music charts, lived on Ha'penny
Brow, Preston, in a terraced house with a wooden gate upon
which was fixed a plywood disc, painted black to resemble a
vinyl disc and, just in case you didn't notice this, it was
modestly named Golden Record Villa.

My own renderings of Calvert's hit probably hastened the
sad demise of the Saturday night church dance, but I never
wondered why there was such a sudden demand for tea in
the next room while I was playing. For me it was the high
point of the evening. I attempted the same two tunes in
public every week, but at home I had the sheet music for
Softly, Softly, with a two-tone picture of the gentle Ruby
Murray on the cover, and *Little Things Mean a Lot* by Joan
Regan. The seeds of showbusiness must have been starting
to germinate at St Leonard's: I got to blow my trumpet and
nothing else mattered.

I was seriously worried one eventful night at St Leonard's
Church Hall when I actually kissed one of the girls. I think
I interfered with her bosom – although, on reflection, it
was not a deliberate interference, it was almost unavoidable – and I was worried sick what the reprisals would be.
The church social was not a place for bosom-touching and
I don't think a lot of that went on among my friends. At
fifteen or sixteen we didn't touch one another anywhere
else, that's for sure!

The classic story of a 50s teenager goes: I remember my
first sexual experience very clearly – I was eleven (I was on
my own at the time!). These days you don't need church
socials; you could just go round the back of the building and

be as naughty as you both like. I'm not sure that things have altered for the better, but the young people I know seem to have a fairly healthy, well balanced idea about sex, and they do it together very much more than we did. Mr Happy wasn't too happy; we really didn't know what it was about. We didn't half miss out. What wasted years!

Serving in the newsagent's at Padiham brought me into direct eye contact with a wonderful variety of ladies' lumps. By the time I was fourteen I'd built up enough courage to ask out a girl who wore a white sweater that really got me going. I arranged to meet her on a bridge at lunchtime. God knows what I intended to do with her at fourteen. Perhaps I intended to meet her, walk across the bridge and go out with her for 200 yards. I don't even remember her name, but I do remember the feeling of being stood up, walking back and forth across the bridge in nervous anticipation, then being told by a friend who happened to pass by, 'You might as well go home, Jim. She told me she wasn't going to turn up!'

This was the first of a number of rebuffs which I blamed on my glasses. Try as I might, and I did try, girls never featured in my life until I had less time to think about them.

I must have been fairly responsible by the time I was fifteen because I remember Mum and Dad went away to Blackpool leaving me to look after the shop by myself. I rose to the occasion and felt particularly privileged to be left in charge of the off-licence part of the business.

It was about this time that I had an unusually strained conversation with my Uncle Arthur. Dad and I never had a man-to-man talk about anything, least of all lumps and ladies, and he must have arranged to delegate that delicate subject to my nautical uncle. Well-intentioned, maybe, but totally ineffective; I was so surprised that my mind went blank and I didn't take in any of this precious information he offered. I just remember seeing my uncle's normally jovial face pulled into a strangely serious expression, with a succession of new and unintelligible words coming out of it ... 'Birds and bees passing ships in the night without washing private parts with care ... be prepared for dangerous fumblings which could delay events on ladies' calendars.'

Any link between calendars and birds and bees sailing on ships passing in the dark without navigational aids and being in need of cleansing was beyond me. I took in absolutely nothing. Uncle Arthur's well-meaning lecture rendered me paralysed with embarrassment, so I hurriedly began sorting newspapers on the shop counter, praying for a customer to come in and divert Uncle Arthur's flow on to something more comprehensible like the price of half a pound of margarine. I could answer *that* question.

Salvation came in the form of a grubby five-year-old with two pennies in his hand for an ice lolly. So at fifteen I still thought that if you played with any part of a lady she became pregnant.

I was also naive about schoolwork. I had worked at school but I didn't realize how to study or how to concentrate. It's important that during those early teen years there's someone who makes you believe in yourself, believe you can succeed and gives you the incentive to want to get it right, to want to win and not to compromise. But there were no Misses Pilkington around for me then.

I wanted to pass my O-levels, but I simply didn't know that I wasn't concentrating. I hadn't experienced success at grammar school, so I had no experience of achieving to draw upon. Maths, especially, meant little to me until later, when I met a teacher called Miss Birtwell. So in 1953, the same year that Dad went to Wembley to see Blackpool beat Bolton Wanderers 4–3 in what became known as the Stanley Matthews Final, and came home with a story about sitting next to Mr Ellis, the FA Cup Final referee, on the London Underground, I was faced with GCE O-level exams with precious little understanding of what I had to do to pass them.

I thought my trumpet and my running were coming along nicely, but I tended to lack interest in many lessons, particularly in biology, where under the kindly and undisciplined auspices of a Mr Wilson, I'm afraid I liked to put little drops of acid on frogs to watch them jump. I convinced myself that I had revised for my exams when I had really only thought about it. Armed with the certain knowledge that $HCl + H_2O + frog = $ maximum jumps, I took eight O-levels and failed nine. My parents were devastated. There was no showdown at home, but Dad had his own way of telling me when something was wrong – he sulked for weeks and brought an atmosphere of gloom into the house which Mum managed to handle very well by carrying on as normal, or so I thought. She was very steady and unflappable – and she smoked cigarettes with gusto.

With no qualifications whatsoever, I saw no alternative but to leave school and get myself a job. I had a dismal premonition that my trumpet was about to take a back seat.

6

Ashes to Academia

I taught myself to tie half a Windsor knot, so I could manage as far as the first over-and-under and get an asymmetrical triangle festooning my Adam's apple, but I had to devote a lot of time on the school bus to mastering the second movement, the up-and-under. Once I had a good Windsor knot in place I was so insecure about it that I left it in place for future use. It was never untied; every Saturday night I would ease down the knot and slip the tie over my head, so my chin gradually wore away the pattern on the same triangle of cloth until it was so frayed that it had to be thrown away having lived all its life in the one ever-darker knot that had been tied on the school bus.

Another essential element of the acceptable teenage image in those days was Brylcreem, which gave me a sleek 'Tony Curtis' (the name we gave to DAs, the pointy bit of the hairline at the nape of the neck resembling the aft formation of a duck's feathers) and one of the most upstanding front waves at the Brier Ballroom in Brierfield. I liked to imagine that the sparkles of light from the revolving mirrored globe reflected on the shiny black hair, the deep sheen of my royal-blue barathea suit and the oxblood-polished shine on my shoes, crêpe-soled of course. Nice smart appearance, shame about the face, the mirror told me when I put on my best Tony Curtis smile.

My other accoutrements in the summer of 1953 were a toning blue shirt and blue tie, which, I was assured by further lengthy communications with the mirror in my bedroom, were designed to send the girls into a frenzy. The mirror lied to me.

Every Saturday night I took the bus to Brierfield along with the in-crowd at the St Leonard's youth club, to dance the night away to a four-piece band playing quicksteps such as *One o'Clock Jump*, foxtrots such as *Sentimental Journey* and waltzes such as *Tammy*. The Brier band's rendition of *Tammy* sounded nowhere near as good as Debbie Reynolds'; it sounded safe. The same numbers were played in the same order every week, which was reassuring because I knew the best moment to ask a girl to dance.

By far the riskiest dance of the evening was the cha-cha, with the samba a less intense second. In the style of the day these dances involved bodily movements verging on the suggestive, bottoms wagging furiously and tops swaying in unison. I was confident that my own protuberance went unnoticed, probably because I was too frightened to join in the dance.

I never got the chance to confirm or disprove my notion that you could make babies by touching ladies' lumps, because I always got the cold shoulder from any girl I dared to draw close to my Windsor knot.

Conversations during the last waltz went something like this: 'Where do you live?'

'Nelson.'

'Can I take you home?'

'No, I've got me friend wi' me.'

Or: 'No, me dad's picking me up.'

Or: 'No, I've a bus to catch.'

Or: 'No, I'm not a girl like that, I'm going the other way.' I was never quite sure what that meant.

I couldn't pull a ligament!

So every Saturday night I took the bus back to Padiham. I remember distinctly the atmosphere of the Saturday-night bus, unlike the feeling on the same bus on any other night of the week. The upper deck was unheated except by clouds of cigarette smoke, and there was a faint, familiarly welcoming smell of alcohol. A stupefied contentment settled over the passengers as soon as they climbed aboard. I sat at the back of the bus whenever possible and there was a metal plate on the seat in front to remind me to take care when raising my head.

On arriving home I'd creep up to my bedroom, alone again, hang up the suit, slip off the tie, taking care not to unfasten the Windsor knot, and examine the shirt to decide whether it warranted a wash. Almost invariably my activities during the evening had not even caused the shirt to crease, so it usually hung under my suit ready for the next assault on the ladies of the Brier Ballroom.

Alas, the elusive perils of the cha-cha were not enough to lift me from the state of mindlessness that had descended on my daily routine since leaving school.

I remember the name of my careers officer, but I won't use it. True, I lacked GCE subjects, direction, motivation, and quite clearly had no idea at all about what path I was to take in the wide world of industry, and it may be that he dealt with me on a bad day. Nevertheless, his performance level was subterranean.

Under his guidance, I gratefully accepted a job as a laboratory assistant at the mill, where I began to plot a collar-and-tie future in the cotton industry. When I was asked to leave after six weeks, I discovered that the careers officer had omitted to tell me that this had always been a temporary appointment. He should have known what a blow this would be to a boy going on sixteen, but he could not have foreseen the wrath that was to fall on my head from Dad. In my father's eyes having a contract terminated meant that I had been sacked; I had failed yet again.

I walked home on the Friday with my employment card in my pocket and was preparing to face what I knew was going to be two at the very least disappointed parents. Bearing in mind Dad had worked all his life, never having put a foot wrong, nay having always stayed on the up, I knew that my apparent dismissal was going to be a very bitter pill for him to swallow. I was absolutely correct.

'What do you mean you've got your cards? No one gets their cards for nothing!' He glowered in a way that brooked no argument.

'It's always been a temporary job,' I tried to explain. 'But nobody told me.'

This was no panacea to my parents. I had been sacked, dismissed, sent home, it was the beginning of a returned empty syndrome.

I felt bitterly let down, and my memory of that incident gives me a lot of sympathy for young people on the Youth Training Schemes of today – working for up to two years without proper pay and knowing that there's no job at the end of it must be a very hard way to grow up. The economics of the 50s were very different: there wasn't much money about, but there was plenty of work. The normal way of life was to have a job; 'unemployment' wasn't a word in common parlance and to be 'out of work' meant you were either lazy or disabled. When I lost the job in the labs, the only thing to be done was to find another one the same week and get on with it. That's how it was in those days – there wasn't a lot of thinking to be done, you could more or less walk into town and say, 'I'll take that job.' I don't even remember what I did with the money I earned, which was probably two or three pounds a week.

The shifty careers officer didn't merit another visit or even another thought, he had become a complete non-event. I count him as the first of the few people I've met in my life whom I choose to obliterate from my personal reality. He no longer existed for me as a real person; he had become a member of the small number of complete wassocks I've met in my life whom I classify as the Obliterati.

I went to Padiham Town Hall to see Mr Hewitt, the

sanitary inspector for Padiham Urban District Council, no less, and incidentally father of my Brier Ballroom pal Sam, who had got himself a place at Leeds University even though I never thought he demonstrated a very intelligent use of Brylcreem.

'Excuse me, Mr Hewitt, sorry to trouble you, but I find myself quite unexpectedly available for work of any kind. Are there any opportunities in your department for a sixteen-year-old to work?' I was just sixteen and felt this entitled me to a man's job.

I must have made an impression. The following Monday morning I took on a new role in life as an apprentice dustbinman.

It was a hardy life 'on the bins'. A six o'clock start on a freezing cold morning emptying dustbins in the days before bin liners was not an experience for the faint-hearted, but I was glad to be there, having made such a mess of everything else. The dustbinmen were a characterful crew, mostly in their fifties and sixties. As the youngest member of the team I was automatically allocated the junior post inside the dustcart, which meant that I spent my days standing in the back of the van, catching the dustbins and emptying them. They didn't have compressors – I was the compressor.

My feet moved rhythmically over the old marmalade jars, fag ends and piles of ashes from the fire grates of Padiham. Different streets offered no variety, because the ashes coloured everything a uniform rust colour, dusting over all class distinction between the rubbish of Padiham's haves and have-nots. Most bins were cursorily searched for treasure, such as the odd wearable cardigan or a discarded jacket of some quality. The rules governing conduct of behaviour concerning contents of dustbins were non-existent; not for us the bottle bank, orange or green, because we owned everything we found, thereby widening the scope of our treasure trove.

I was going home, sitting in the bath and thinking, 'Well something else might turn up, and I can always do the

Christmas post.' My unhygienic physical state on my return home didn't bother me at first, because I was just glad to be in work. Being given my cards at the job in the mill laboratories had briefly but completely annihilated any sense of ambition I might have had, even as a failed fifth former.

I was by now forming a vision of how my performance must have been affecting my father, who had nurtured the child he'd picked up as a bundle of rags in Liverpool and encouraged it to seize the opportunities he'd never had himself. He was watching that child about to grow into a man while squandering his abilities and taking the job of a dustbinman from someone who needed it. It was a big learning curve for me, but my father communicated more and more with shrugging shoulders and dark looks.

Weekday evenings were long and glum. Dad would sit in his cushioned chair with bentwood arms, reading a newspaper and listening to the radio that sat on the big redwood sideboard with its oval mirror and decorative plinths. Mum had a high-backed chair by the table with its velveteen cloth and I would lounge on the settee in my own world, waiting for my weekly sortie to the Brier Ballroom. Occasionally, if I carefully picked the right moment, I could elicit a low chuckle from Dad by doing an impersonation of the comedian Al Read. I would always agree with Dad when he said he didn't like Vic Oliver, one of the funnymen on 'Variety Bandbox'. Any opinion I held at that time was received from Dad and his moodiness did not lessen my respect for him at this stage. The radio was a great aid to communication: Dad and I used to look at it together when 'Variety Bandbox' was on the Light Programme.

The one and only time Dad ever hit me was when I noticed that there was some dust on the radio, ran my finger along it and said, 'We'll have to get rid of that cleaner. She's flaming useless!'

Dad was sitting with his back to me, reading a newspaper at the table, and he suddenly swung round and gave me a back-hander. I knew what I'd done wrong. I just left the room and I've been polite to cleaners ever since.

Fathers of few words were the norm rather than the exception. They belonged to a generation who had been brought up with a strict Victorian code of behaviour which left them ill equipped to deal with the emotional scars of two wars. I never had to tramp over bodies in France when I was nineteen and come home to a world where everyone was hiding their grief, so I would never criticize Dad for taking life seriously. I just hope I'm a better communicator, although he didn't need a qualification in counselling to let me know that he was bitterly disappointed at my having wasted the opportunity of gaining qualifications at grammar school.

Although I never heard him speak badly of anybody, he did show respect for people who were successful in business. When Mrs Hargreaves, wife of the Managing Director of Padiham Cotton and Cotton Waste Company Ltd came into the shop Dad's manner was somewhat more attentive than when an unshaven no-hoper came in clutching an empty bleach bottle and asking for half a pint of bitter.

It took me nearly two months as a dustbinman to realize that this was not a job I wanted to do for the rest of my life.

The bin team used to have breakfast by the roadside at about seven o'clock in the morning. I had a flask of tea and sandwiches like nothing I've ever tasted since, thankfully. The ash from the coal fires got everywhere, in every crevice and on every eyelash, and however carefully I took my sandwiches out of the paper, there would be dark patches of ash where I'd held the bread with my fingers. If you changed hands while you were eating you digested two perfect sets of fingerprints. I suppose the dietitians would call it roughage.

One morning when I was eating my customary ash sandwich, gaffer said something that jolted me into realizing that there was more to life than marmalade on my boots.

The gaffer was a wise old bird who supervised everything; he decided who was walking up which path to which house (the more rewarding were his) and he delegated the tipping and compressing responsibilities on the basis of the biggest boots being the best for compressing with. He was contemplating his colourful bread and roughage one winter morning when, apropos of nothing, he fixed his eyes on the middle distance and announced, 'When you think how long this world has been turning and how long it's likely to go on turning, we're only here for a bloody weekend.'

I wrapped up that thought and took it away with me, and it became a turning point. It sounds dramatic, but there are certain moments in life when you become super-focused and perception of everything around and within is heightened. This was one of those moments, so I can still taste the ash on my marmalade sandwich, see the gaffer's breath in the frosty air, and feel that new sense of self-determination. My next step in life became clear to me: 'Right, I've had enough of this, I'm going back to school.'

I knew my former-classmates from Accrington Grammar were working their way to college and university. I had already been left behind, but I could catch the next train; I cornered my dad in the back of the shop one evening and swallowed my pride.

'Look Dad, I'm really sorry about all this. If I go back to school will you keep me for another year?'

'Back to school to do what?' was his scathing response.

'To do my GCEs again. I promise I'll work . . .'

'I'm not saying anything about it. If you're really determined to go back, ask your headmaster if he'll take you back after spending a year on the dustbins. If he'll have you back at school, we'll take it from there.' That was as supportive a response as a cigarette-smoking dustbinman son could have hoped for.

Before I returned to school I was moved sideways at work to a different job with the sanitation department, from the wild collection to the disciplined selection of waste. I became a waste-paper packer. The new job brought in an extra couple of quid a week because I was paid by the bale. It was one of the most economic and environmentally friendly waste disposal systems that ever came into existence in Padiham, for it had been decided that money could be made from taking cardboard out of rubbish. All the recycling stations and bottle banks you see around Lancashire today are undoubtedly a result of my pioneering work in recycling. I had to ram the waste paper down into a metal thresh and each time I picked up a heap of paper rats were liable to leap out in every direction. Although there was a thinner coating of dirt and grime washed off in the bath at the end of the day, it didn't feel like a promotion because there were far more rats involved in the work, but at least I was diversifying. I was working at the side of the tip where the dustcarts emptied all the rubbish, so I had seen the job from both ends of the marmalade jar. I could do the job because I knew I didn't have to do it for ever, as I was determined to get back on the academic roundabout as soon as possible. There had to be more to my life than ash-laden butties.

I knew I had never made much of an impression on headmaster Ben Johnson, but now was the moment. I walked through the dark wooden doors of Accrington Grammar School and was ridiculously pleased to recognize the soapy smell and the familiar red hair of the lumpless Miss Holden, the school secretary whom I spoke to through a hatch.

'Oh, it's Whittaker.' She remembered my name, at least.

'Hello, Miss Holden, how are you?'

She looked confused and adjusted her serious spectacles.

'Can I see the boss? Can I see Mr Johnson please?' I could smell pipe smoke, so I knew he was in there.

She dropped the hatch, I heard mumbling, then Johnson's tweedy baritone, 'Whittaker, come in!' The door opened.

Ben Johnson glowered at me over his horn rims and nodded towards an empty chair. I hadn't expected a welcome-back party.

'How can I help you, Whittaker?' he asked, but he knew – and I knew – how much I needed his help.

I took a deep breath and my well-rehearsed words tumbled

out in a rush. 'Sir, I'd like to take my GCEs again.'

'You're sixteen, lad, and I'm not having you in the sixth form.'

'No, sir. May I go back into the fifth year, sir?'

'You're not going into 5A.'

'I know, sir. I'd be delighted to go into 5B, if that's all right, sir?' I said, thinking, Don't be too proud to beg or it's back to the rats and recycling.

'Are you working now?'

I nodded.

'Then I'll risk it,' said Johnson. 'You can join 5B in September.'

'Thank you. Thank you very much, sir.'

The remaining weeks of waste-paper selection were purely filling in time before my return to school, which I was looking forward to immensely. There was light at the end of the tunnel and I knew I'd been given a chance to redeem my complete and utter balls-up. With a goal to look forward to, I worked among the rats with a lighter heart. I was on my way. I wanted a collar-and-tie job, as a schoolteacher, and to that end I was determined to pass my O-levels.

7

Returned Empty

When I squeezed myself behind a small school desk in September 1954, it didn't matter to me that I was a head taller than most of my classmates. My year away from school in the world of work had given me a strong sense of purpose. I knew why I was there and I was very glad to be back.

My contemporaries were now in the Upper Sixth and lording it as prefects, but I was treated exactly like the rest of 5B. Our form teacher in room 17 was the Physics master, W. R. Acklam, fondly known as Daddy Ack. Everybody loved him. He was a fine little man, four foot nothing, never been bricked, and I think he had taught Florence Nightingale first aid in 1840. When I walked in on the first day of term he looked at me and he said, 'Ah, here's another returned empty,' but he said it in such a jovial, friendly way that I wanted to pass everything to please him. I was on the way back. The other returned empties had done resits in November, whereas I was a very late, very incongruous return. Funny, from handling returned empties on the dustcart to becoming one myself!

Faced with the challenge of sitting with boys who were two academic years behind me, I was determined to be top of that class. I also wanted to set 5B an example and inspire the class to avoid acting like also-rans and getting themselves into the situation I'd found myself in the year before. With my new-found sense of direction I even looked forward to homework. I studied hard every evening with the picture of myself as a teacher at the front of my mind and a picture of myself as a dustman at the back of my mind to spur me on. My work was immaculately neat and I consistently earned full marks. If I saw marks of less than nine out of ten in my homework book I was destroyed; I was so intent on getting everything right that an eight and a half was a catastrophe.

Mr Wilson, the gentle biology teacher, now saw a transformed student. My biology diagrams were works of art, and there were never any discipline problems in his class because I was big enough to keep the other kids quiet. No one dared consider going near the frogs with acid because I'd give them a good coating (telling orff) and say, 'Eh, cut that out. I want to pass this subject.'

With Miss Birtwell, the maths teacher, I grasped the thorns of calculus and trigonometry and handed in diagrams she described as 'exquisite' – I was the dog's bollocks. In Daddy Ack's class I came top all year and was determined to get an A in the exam. Something had clicked, the penny had dropped – I had learned how to study and sat at the little table in my bedroom every evening knowing I was giving it my best shot.

With my new-found confidence came more extrovert behaviour. When the school's mock elections were set up, with Labour and Conservative candidates chosen from potential public speakers in the Upper Sixth, my classmates in 5B encouraged me to stand. 'Why don't you have a go, Jim? You're taller than the other candidates and we'll support you.'

Having precious little understanding of politics or elections, I decided to ask the advice of the music master, George Crick. I didn't study music but I chose him because he seemed an approachable sort of character. I had noticed sounds of ribaldry and chaos drifting from his lessons in the school hall. Most of Mr Crick's pupils couldn't tell a treble clef from a cartoon cat.

'Would it be easier to stand for Labour or Conservative?' I asked.

'You can't stand for either of the main parties because the candidates are already chosen,' George Crick explained.

'Are there any other parties then?' I persisted.

'You could stand as an Independent candidate . . .' mused the music master, giving me a hint of a conspiratorial grin.

'That sounds good. What does an Independent candidate do that a Conservative one can't?'

'He can vote for himself. He doesn't have to vote with the party.'

That settled it for me. The 5B-ites became my party workers and after some confusion over the spelling of 'Independent', posters went up all over the school proclaiming, 'Be Independent. Vote for Jim.' I was very proud of them; this was my first, naïve attempt at showbusiness. I was determined to twinkle.

The Conservative candidate was Anthony Portno, who was also the son of the deputy head and on his way to Oxbridge. I knew he was my main opposition. As an ex-dustbinman, I also knew that my speech would have to be good. The 5-Bummites were right behind me (pardon me) and again I enlisted the help of Mr Crick. I thought it was the best speech I'd ever written – it was the only speech I'd ever written.

Ben Johnson wanted the speeches to be serious and well-researched, but I rose to the podium and turned the hustings into a piece of light entertainment. My speech got laughs. In fact my speech got the only laughs. Anthony Portno looked worried and beat me by two votes – not a heart-warming result for headmaster Ben Johnson, who considered it to be very poor reflection on the school. When a local newspaper reporter came to compile a small article, Mr Johnson felt it necessary to comment that a certain candidate had gained votes because of his personality rather than his policies, which were not in line with those of the school (or of any political party known to man).

The bundle of rags exposed on receipt.

The Accrington Cowboy, 1939. Mum watching me set off on a long journey across the back yard at 303 Dill Hall Lane.

Our dog Bess with Mum outside our 17-hour-a-day shop in Padiham.

Action shot of Mum and Dad on the prom at Blackpool. Photo by Bowen, née Whittaker, née Williams, aged 9.

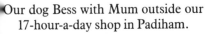

With Phyllis outside the Golden Garter, Manchester, 1971. My name in lights for the first time at a premier cabaret venue.

Just after our son Pete's christening in 1974 – how we've aged!

We were in the army together, but by this time Bobby Charlton was a legend and I was still struggling to make a mark.

I think George Crick had enjoyed helping me present such an unacceptable face of school politics, particularly as he was a personal friend of Ben Johnson. (I knew this because I'd seen them having classical jam sessions on the piano in the school hall at lunchtimes.) What the mock election gave me was my first experience of getting laughs from 700 people in a hall.

'That was a good speech, Jim,' said Walter Waine, my history master. 'You have a sense of timing; you ought to go into showbusiness.'

One of the seeds was sown, but Walter's words left me slightly confused because he was a very quiet, studious sort of man and I was shocked at his compliment on my extrovert style.

My only other opportunity to perform before a school audience came with my memorable contribution to the school play, produced by Flossy Ferguson. I played a vital crowd member in George Bernard Shaw's *The Devil's Disciple*. I conscientiously attended every rehearsal and learned my lines diligently. I was on stage for about twenty seconds and extended my appearance for another three seconds by sticking my head around the curtain on my way off stage. When my mathematics teacher, Miss Birtwell, had seen the play she said to me, 'You mean to tell me you missed twelve lessons of maths just to say, "Get him!"?'

It was true. I only had two words to say but I wanted to be part of the theatrical scene. And Miss Birtwell knew I wasn't neglecting my maths because I wanted to study the subject at teacher training college.

I had been accepted at Chester College of Education on condition that I passed my O-levels, and I was actually looking forward to the exams; I wanted to get on with my life because I now saw a clear route to teaching.

Two years earlier when I had walked into the same exam rooms and turned over the sheets of printed question papers I had been ill-prepared. This time I had been focusing on that moment for a year; the exam questions made sense this time, I knew what was expected of me and so I was calmer and more confident. After each exam I had a satisfied feeling that told me I'd done well, so in the summer of 1955 I awaited my exam results with impatience.

When the day came to go into school to pick up the results, I put on my school blazer for the last time and strode out into the sunshine, confident of qualifying for teacher training college. What a difference two years had made!

Ben Johnson was handing out the results and as soon as I saw his face I knew I'd done well. There was a smile on his face, a twinkle in his dark eyes and the deep lines in his brow shrank to gentle wrinkles.

'Congratulations, Whittaker, you got the lot,' he said. 'And most of them are As.'

I ran home hoping for a bigger reaction from Dad than the one I got when I had passed my 11-plus all those years before. Isn't it peculiar that through all this period of my life I was more concerned about getting it right for my father when really Mum had more than earned the right to be considered first? It was she who, like my wife Phyllis now, bore the brunt of running the household and looking after its members without complaint of any kind. But, as they say in Lancashire, I had a head like a forty-shilling guzunder.

My father's response was not effusive, but he was obviously pleased that I was going to be a teacher and he bought me a new trumpet. I do remember feeling that he had always known I could do it, that deep down he had trusted me to put things right and get myself a good job eventually.

Having made the necessary effort, I knew I would now have a choice of jobs, unlike the students of today who have to find the self-discipline and motivation to pass exams in the expectation of no job, no wage, nothing. Luckily I was able to turn my life around in 1955. At fifteen I had been a dustman with no O-levels; at seventeen I had nine O-levels and had been accepted for a teacher training course. Before I could take up my place at Chester Church of England Teacher Training College I decided to get the compulsory two years of National Service out of the way, so I got an early call-up in order to finish in time to hit Chester for the autumn term of 1957.

Learning how to make changes in my life was a major step. I was determined to make the light at the end of the tunnel even brighter.

And lo, the young James hath gotten up from the ashes whence he came, and stood in, and ate sandwiches in. Henceforth James Brown Whittaker, ex-dustbinman of the parish of Padiham, faceth his future with much conviction and determination.

8

If You Knew Suez

The best way to recall the first day of National Service is as an onlooker. I was stripped, dipped, clipped and equipped amid so much scurrying around and barked orders that I felt obliged to watch the new recruits go through the same process as often as I could during the following two years of service, as a reminder of what I'd survived and also because it was far, far funnier when it was happening to someone else.

For the first time in my life I realized that there was a learning curve in life. Imagine a graph, with the two axes meeting at zero: the vertical axis is the experience gained in terms of 'experions', while the horizontal axis marks the passage of time. Few people would have a smooth, rising curve for their entire life until the day comes when Mr Happy is no longer functioning along with the rest of his surroundings. My two years of National Service was a period where my learning curve shot up from wherever it was at eighteen by at least 10,000 'experions', and most of the upturn happened in the first six weeks at Hilsea barracks in Portsmouth.

I'd travelled down on the train in my barathea suit, glancing sideways at every station the train stopped at to try to identify any other new recruits. But it would have been foolish to try and make new friends on the first day. There was no time.

My suit and suitcase were whisked away and various items of clothing and equipment were thrust into my arms. There was the navy-blue beret that sat on your head like an inverted wok until you had dowsed it in hot and cold water to shrink it into shape; trousers, legs for the covering of; drawers cellular, Mr Happy for the containing of; rifle, enemy for the shooting of; shirts that wouldn't fit a child; socks that reached the armpits; and, of course, the giant boots.

Woe betide anyone who took more than a second to state their boot size. The officer in charge of boot distribution would make a quick guess and lob a pair of boots at any hesitant person. You could spot them the next day on parade, slipping about inside a spare inch or two of boot space or wincing at the blisters.

Later we would play Spot the Camel Marchers if we had a moment to watch new recruits coming to terms with their feet. There were always the natural non-marchers to look out for. Some people find it impossible to swing the opposite arm to the forward leg and the more they try the more ungainly and camel-like their marching becomes.

My six weeks of basic training at Hilsea barracks, Portsmouth were as nothing to what the commandos get in the marines, but it was a hell on earth that I wouldn't have missed for the world. We learned the meaning of words, expressions, experiences and emotions that no other aspect of our lives to date had given us. Words like discipline, order, regimentation, obedience; expressions such as blind obedience, awareness of your fellow man, sheer terror; experiences of carrying out orders you didn't believe were right, obeying someone you didn't agree with, doing things you really didn't want to do and doing them without question. Within two days of my entrance to Hilsea barracks all that began to make sense.

I was absolutely terrified of a five-foot-two Sergeant Shelton, a man I could have eaten in a pub, who asked me to paint coal white, and who upset my bed because he said a knife that was three degrees off the vertical made it untidy.

Standing on guard duty for two hours on, four hours off, on the freezing cold nights when we couldn't feel the butts of our rifles was no picnic, but there was a purpose, even though our rifles were empty and we were guarding an empty wooden shed, worth a total of £3.50 at today's MFI prices. We had to stare into the dark for two hours in case anyone came towards the shed and we had to shout, 'Halt. Who goes there?' How stupid can you get? But what happy memories and how that learning curve shot up!

We learned about comradeship, we learned how to support and help our fellow men, some of whom were having great difficulty coming to terms with the regime after the freedom of places like Brier Ballroom, where the trombone player didn't even finish at the same time as the rest of the band. We marched in groups of thirty to nowhere and back, we moved rifles across our bodies in unison for hours, we polished boots for hours, using heated teaspoons to melt away any pimples of polish and achieve the obligatory faultless shine.

In the context of National Service excellence sometimes meant showing a guy that there's only one way to polish a pair of boots so they gleam until they can gleam no more. You can't understand the feeling of satisfaction and well-being you get after you've done a five-mile bash with a hundred-pound pack on your back unless some little sergeant whose parents were unmarried makes you do it in the first place and urges you on with verbal laxatives.

I regarded Sergeant Shelton with great respect and affection by the time I left Hilsea barracks to go to the ROAC School of Ammunition at Bramley in Hampshire. In the Ordnance Corps if you could put your cap on the right way round you were an academic, but I'd only got my GCE O-levels second time around so I didn't get a commission. I did get on the 233A/E course at Bramley to train as an ammunitions examiner, one of the three trades in the army that carried two stripes. This meant I had to sign the Official Secrets Act and be on call until I was forty-five, by which time

I'd have been as useful to World War Three as a chocolate fireguard.

My nine months of intensive ammunitions training involved bomb disposal, identifying and servicing equipment, recognizing different strengths of explosives and knowing which way to run when you had a detonator in your hand. I got through the highly technical parts because I got one mark more than the guy below me, and I think he was failed because they had run out of places at the Central Ammunition Depot at Nescliffe in Shrewsbury, where I was posted as a corporal and which I believe is now a pleasant housing estate.

I was to work as an ammunitions examiner, checking over ammunition stores and protecting the river Severn from the English side, and defending the nation against the Welsh.

My biggest coup in terms of the quality of life was persuading the RSM to allocate a Nissen hut as a band room. I thought I was simply looking for a way of making life more fun, but in retrospect I can see I was developing my ability of feeling for the chemistry of a situation. I intuitively knew if I was handling somebody the right way and knew that the easiest way to get what I wanted from the RSM was to admit I had got something wrong, then immediately he would be falling over himself to help me with his superior knowledge. Enabling other people to contribute their skills to my project was a useful exercise in man management.

My trumpet playing was, as now, less than mediocre, but I found a drummer and a very good saxophone player who got hold of the Jimmy Lally arrangements for tunes like *Fascination*, *Memories of You* and *Blue Moon*. We learned ten or twelve tunes altogether, including quicksteps and waltzes, then we were ready to entertain. The RSM hated academics, but he liked the music and he liked even more the idea that he had organized us. He even got us two half-days a week off to rehearse in the band room, which was a nice little perk. I suppose even then there was showbusiness in me because I wouldn't rest until we'd played for a dance in the officers' mess and been asked back for a repeat performance by popular demand.

This was my first opportunity to stand on a stage for a long time and show off by playing my trumpet and telling gags. I loved it, although entertaining was never part of my career plan at this point; I was going to be a teacher and the idea of even mentioning showbusiness to my father was unthinkable.

We kept the band going all the time I was at the Central Ammunition Depot at Nescliffe, which meant I was always excused from parade there.

I heard that most of the big camps in Aldershot had a corporals' mess and so I decided to get one established for the 66 battalion. We definitely needed our own lady instead of having to struggle through the pioneer corps' canteen for a cuppa and I managed to convince the people that mattered that it was another string to the battalion's bow. After all, they had corporals' messes at all the big prestigious camps ...

'Well, I'm sure, sir,' I said to the Sergeant-Major, 'if you worked on the idea and helped us with your expertise we could get the project off the ground. What was it like when you were a corporal, sir?'

'Oh, we had a mess, but times have changed.'

I had him in the palm of my hand. Eventually he even came in to help us organize bingo.

Our first corporals' dance involved a little coercion. I had invited some ladies from a local nursing home, thinking that the mention of live music and thirty corporals who had just come off bromide in their tea would be a big crowd puller. On the night, though, only four girls appeared and one of them looked as if she needed smelling salts. I would be lynched if the bromide-free boys arrived to the prospect of dancing with each other all evening, so I got the service corps driver to take me in the Nescliffe bus to the nursing home, where I stood outside the windows and shouted in a civilized manner: 'Attention! Attention! Safe transport available to and from the hottest dance of the year. Roll up, come as you are, live music, live dancing and transport home ...' until I had filled the coach with nurses. They trusted me. It had something to do with my horn-rimmed spectacles and the desperately shy way I yelled up at their windows.

As we drove back into camp I felt as though I'd cast my net and achieved a little miracle, not with loaves and fishes but with enough lovely nurses with curves for a very successful evening. From four females I had brought forth thirty-four in the twinkling of a trumpet. The band played on and a good night was had by all. It was rumoured that eight corporals volunteered for bromide in excess the next morning.

And so the summer of '56 was passed to the tunes of *Blue Moon* and *Memories Of You* in the band's Nissen hut and the familiar rhythms of ear-bashing from the RSM on the parade ground. In August, however, my peripheral involvement with the Suez crisis led to banishment from the ammunitions department.

The neutrality of the Suez Canal had been guaranteed by the British since 1888, but when the British troops withdrew in 1956 President Nasser nationalized the canal, provoking an Anglo-French attack on Egypt. So our boys needed some ammo. I was detailed to go down to one of the ammunition sheds to send out 3.5in breech-loading high-explosive shells to Suez, via Barry Docks in South Wales. Having checked the dates on the stacks of propellant, I had it all shipped to the docks, believing it to be dated 1947. But I had only looked at the dates on the crates on the outside of the stack and my colleague at the docks spotted that some of those in the middle of the stack were ten years older.

Had my error gone undetected, our lads in Suez might have been firing shells that landed several hundred yards short of the target and I could have been responsible for bombing our own regiments. In fact, nothing much happened so the shells were not needed. The rest of the world judged that the Anglo-French attack on Suez was out of order, so our troops withdrew after a few days and came home with sand in their Vaseline.

Luckily for me, the mistake was corrected and I was quietly removed to a place where there was nothing explosive so I could do no further damage – the Physical Training Instructors' course at Park Hall, Oswestry. If there had been so much as a box of matches at Park Hall I wouldn't have got on the course.

There weren't many PTIs with bad eyes, but they had to do something with me and it had been noted that I was a good runner, especially in the vicinity of a detonator. I didn't excel on the PTI course, but I was in good shape physically and enjoyed coaching. I could coach soccer well even though I was by no means a great player, and I could motivate a guy and encourage him to do a perfect hollow-back hand spring, indeed a hollow-back somersault, without actually doing one myself. Somehow I had the eye for the shape and mechanics of gymnastics, and I enjoyed the coaching.

With no responsibility whatsoever for ammunitions, except my own, they let me back into Nescliffe a month later as an instructor, a PTI. No one could see any exceptional physical ability in me, but I suppose I was a good communicator. I didn't have a problem with rank, so I could express myself and be as outrageous as the army would allow because I got results.

I knew I had a sort of gift for giving people confidence, and that's not a boast, it's just something that I can do and enjoy doing. If someone came to our house tomorrow and said they couldn't swim, I'd want to have them swimming before they left, even though I'm not a keen swimmer myself. Ninety-nine per cent of the time I can do it, even for people with phobias about water, although that might take a bit longer.

During National Service I developed effective words of encouragement and the ability to make people believe in themselves. 'You really can do this. Trust me,' are key words in the learning process. The notion of teaching learning

became a popular philosophy in the 60s, but it was an instinc-
tive knack I discovered in the army against a backcloth of
fear of what would happen if you didn't learn – and learn at
the double.

There was, however, one situation on parade which I
misread badly, thus blowing my chance of another stripe.

'Two to go on a drill course. Whittaker, step forward,'
bawled Captain Guthrie.

A drill course being about as enticing as watching paint
dry, I gave him a quick look and sulked. Seeing my diffidence
he immediately volunteered another corporal. After the
parade warrant officer first class WO1 Brennan , a hard Scot,
sought me out. I had a soft spot for him. He had been in the
army since he was two months old and eventually had great
difficulty in coming to terms with civilian life.

'Why did you slide out of the drill course, Corporal Whittaker?' he asked.

'Sir, I didn't want to do all that marching up and down,
sir.'

'You would have been marching two weeks to three stripes,'
Brennan barked. I think he was more annoyed than I was. I
really couldn't see myself as a sergeant, because alongside
men like Don Wilson, Robbie Catternach and Keith Howells,
who already had degrees, I felt very inadequate with only my
nine O-levels. I tried to make up for my inadequacies by
being outlandish and a motivator. As a human being I left a
lot to be desired, but I was good at finding the fun and I
could turn the heat on and get most people to do things,
with the notable exception of a certain secretary named
Christine.

Visiting home on weekend leave I noticed that the army
uniform camouflaged my spindlier parts and emphasized
those which the PTI course had developed. Even my spectacles looked more interesting, the mirror told me. At any
rate, the uniform seemed to make the ladies at the All Saints
church social want to dance with me, which in turn gave me
new-found confidence that appealed to a certain Christine,

who certainly made my buttons twinkle as they had never twinkled before. She actually turned up for our first date and we soon deserted the church socials in favour of Sunday nights at her mum and dad's house.

Christine's parents used to go out and leave us alone, then fumble noisily with the latch key when they returned. Oh, I did like them. They were a great couple, decent, Christian and understanding. And nicely reckless, I thought, but my moments of teenage passion 50s-style were well spent in making up for lost time kissing and cuddling, and I never got my socks off. In fact I never got anything off, and certainly didn't get Christine off. And after her mother tactfully lowered our blood pressure with tea and biscuits, I'd head briskly for the last bus, adjusting my disturbingly efficient army underpants cellular, Mr Happy for the containing of.

My main enthusiasms remained contained and in waiting in my cellular drawers and my trumpet bag, as I counted the hours to demob day, which came on 1 September 1957. I have never been happier to wear an old suit on a train than when I journeyed to my parents' new home in Harrington Street, Clayton-le-Moors, where I was to spend two weeks before starting my course at Chester College.

I pondered my civilian toecaps at the old dining table, next to the disappointingly docile new washing machine. The bubble and squeak still hit the spot on Mondays and mercifully Mum asked me no questions about Christine, but the very air in the house seemed to move too slowly. My head was full of plans for my own future, in which Mum and Dad and Clayton-le-Moors were to have had no role to play; my horizons were opening and I could see a clear road ahead – which I suppose is exactly how a young man should feel. Only now I know how my parents felt.

I was raring to conduct my life as an adult in the society of the late 1950s. I had gone into National Service at the age of seventeen and came out with the maturity of a twenty-seven-year-old in some areas of my personality. I thought I was grown up, but in other aspects I'm afraid I didn't really grow up until I was about forty. And now I can regress at will.

I had expected that life at an all-male teacher training college would be far less demanding than barrack life and far less exciting than Padiham Church socials, and I was right. Even Mr Happy demanded little in the first term. Christine's parents had exerted none of their encouraging influence upon their daughter to keep in touch with me now that I had a room of my own where I could receive visitors during daylight hours. After her first visit to Chester College of Education she gave me a weird look and said, 'You've changed, Jim.'

I never saw her again. As I had noticed no marked alteration about my person, I could only assume that she couldn't handle my moving from a corporal in uniform to a college boy in a blazer. Well, I much preferred the blazer and I didn't have time to mope. Getting the elbow from Christine gave me a kick start on my studies, but my pride took a little kick as well. Truth to tell I was severely bruised by the loss. But things were to get better: I was soon to meet someone who was to enrich my life beyond my wildest dreams.

9

Meeting My Future

Only a clown deserts his partner to dance alone with a candle in the breast pocket of his best jacket and a chrysanthemum between his teeth. But for this clown it turned out to be a very lucky solo tango indeed, because it won me a sudden smile from the girl with the most beautiful, steady blue eyes in the room. If not for that smile, my student days would have been solitary and uneventful, and the rest of my life . . . well, I simply cannot imagine it without Phyllis.

The possibility of finding a wife at an all-male college seemed remote, but I was one of the lucky ones. Phyllis and I met in my first term at Chester College of Education and, on reflection, I put more energy into our courtship than the college course.

Since resolving to pass my O-levels I had looked forward to the opportunity to gain a professional qualification. I already had one very useful string to my teaching bow as a qualified physical training instructor, courtesy of Her Majesty's forces, and considerable confidence in crowd control. When I took up my place to study Mathematics and Geography I looked upon my rectangular desk in the rectangular little room in the halls of residence as a means to an end. The purpose of student life in the late 1950s was clear – there was a job and a house at the end of it. Those of us who had already completed National Service were resigned to getting

this second stint of training over with as quickly as possible
in order to begin work in the real world.

Beatniks and bohemians had not been discovered at
Chester College of Education. Although a few arts students
made rebellious statements with beards and briar pipes,
smart college scarves and shiny shoes were the norm. I
habitually began each morning with a vigorous shoe polishing
exercise, which I managed to cut down to a civilian level,
genuinely looking forward to a day that began with a canteen
breakfast of prunes and porridge. In the late 1950s college
life was about getting it all done, rather than letting it all
hang out. You just didn't have the opportunity to let anything
hang out. Female attributes were largely out of sight and out
of the question, and receded to blips in my imagination.

The nearest collection of girls wore the untouchable purple
capes of St Katharine's College of Education, Taggart
Avenue, Liverpool 17, alias The Purple Virgins. I sometimes
saw groups of them swirling around Chester town centre,
taking up far too much room in the bookshops and looking
terribly confident and athletic around the legs. Above the
knee they appeared strangely shapeless and camouflaged,
somehow chaperoned by those billowing tents of purple wool.
I certainly never spotted a purple cape that struck me as
sufficiently short-sighted to contemplate a date with someone
wearing spectacles as thick as mine.

So when the Principal of St Katharine's College extended
the customary invitation to the men of Chester College to
team up with those of her girls who were without partners
from home for the Christmas ball, I went along with inten-
tions more festive than flirtatious. No sooner was I introduced
to my partner – about whom I remember very little apart
from the fact that we felt an instant indifference to one
another – than my pal Laurie Lacey and I were crisply ordered
to move some chairs into the hall. To make the furniture
moving more fun we began the job in a slow military march
formation. My unfortunate partner was watching and I
noticed that it made her face curdle, whereas her friend in

the blue dress looked slightly amused, so we continued with the marching game until all the chairs were in place.

The dancing was all formal ballroom business and my partner was so unimpressed that she rarely deigned to take the floor, which is probably why I was inspired to do my solo interpretation of the tango, with candle in pocket and flower in teeth, by this time caring very little what any of the purple capes thought about me.

Perhaps because Phyllis found my tango irresistible, although she insists it was because I made her laugh, we changed partners so that I danced with Phyllis, and she invited me to join a group of people who were treated to robust sandwiches which she'd had the foresight to prepare in her room. I loved her sandwiches to pieces and was delighted to spend the evening with Phyllis because she enjoyed a bit of fun and festivity. A year younger than me, she was in her second year at college and I gradually found out that she was a great sportswoman – she was games captain at school, an excellent tennis and hockey player, a strong swimmer and a superb all-round athlete. The day after the Christmas ball I thought many times of her soft blue eyes – at once twinkling and trusting. And they have been with me every day since, be it across the country or across the room.

I've sometimes been asked to describe our first meeting, our courtship and our wedding, as if they might contain secret ingredients that have kept our marriage together for thirty-five years, which is regarded as an unusual feat in my business. But I'm simply not a romantic – my heart didn't leap, no birds sang, it was not a dramatic encounter and yet I sensed immediately how amazingly lucky I was to have found Phyllis. From our first meeting there was a rightness about us; it seemed the most natural thing in the world that we should become partners for life. I felt that we were part of each other. And if I cannot find words to express why Phyllis is the strongest, most tender and most beautiful part of my life, it's not because I'm illiterate or short of words, it's just that attempting to put a verbal description on her value to me would be futile. The lady is priceless.

Fortunately Phyllis met my mother a few times and they got along well, but she never knew her as the gentle, sprightly Annie. I wish they had met before my mother fell ill.

In my first year at college Mum was diagnosed as suffering from cancer of the stomach. Dad had told me she was ill, but I don't think I realized just how ill. It could be that everyone remembers their last piece of petulant, childish behaviour before a parent dies, but I wish I didn't. I recall tying my tie in front of a mirror in the living room, having a bit of trouble and yanking it undone to start again (Windsor knots were still a challenge). When Mum leaned out of her chair to try and help me with it, I brushed her away sharply.

'Oh leave me alone, Mum, will you?' I snapped. How insensitive can you get! Dad looked at me with the most severe admonition I'd ever seen in his eyes and I felt ashamed of myself. Christ, why did I talk to her like that? I thought, but I don't remember saying anything to put it right; at that moment I couldn't undo the harsh words.

A far happier memory, also from the time when I didn't properly appreciate what a short time Mum had left to live, was when I went shopping for a suitably high-seated chair so that she could stand up from a sitting position without draining every ounce of energy she had. I searched high and low for a chair to fit the bill until I found a dark green one with wooden arms, which we gave to her for Christmas. She liked that – and we would have known if she hadn't.

Mum's condition deteriorated so quickly and horribly that I dreaded seeing the change in her on my weekend visits home to Clayton-le-Moors.

Her suffering still haunts me as a great injustice, and when the end came in 1958, it did not seem like a blessing. It was a horribly violent end to a most gentle life. The Rev. Ken Houghton stood uncomfortably in the quietened house, supposedly on a visit to comfort my father and me, and pronounced, 'God moves in a mysterious way.' And I hated him. I knew the phrase from the words of the hymn I'd learned without the help of a surplice as a boy at All Saints and it meant absolutely nothing to me. If it meant something to Ken Houghton, why couldn't he explain it better? That was his job after all. The vicar's chosen words of compassion to the bereaved husband and son felt like a kick in the stomach.

Dad clenched his jaw and wrapped his grief tightly around him. As was to be expected, he suffered in silence.

The memory-movie that ran in my own mind was of Mum helping me to learn to ride a two-wheeler bike in the cemetery. It was a quiet place where I could practise without an audience. Time and again I wobbled and fell off as soon as Mum let go of the saddle. 'Never mind, we'll come back again tomorrow. You'll get it right sooner or later, and you never forget once you've learned,' she had said. Mum had never grown impatient, never teased me when I kept falling off the bicycle. She just smiled happily the day I got the knack and sped off around the tracks.

I comforted myself with memories of the moments when I had known Mum was proud of me. When she waved me off to Hilsea barracks for the first time, I'm sure she was afraid I'd never come back home. It sounds melodramatic but it was only ten years after the Second World War and she'd seen other young men go off in uniform and never return. I also remember the look of joy on her face when I came back home to Harrington Street after my six weeks of basic training. I must have looked a right sprog in my hairy khaki uniform, with my dark blue army beret stuck on my head like a stiff pancake and many unintentional creases all over my person.

Mum's pride was even greater when I came home ten months later as a corporal with correctly creased uniform, highly polished brasses and boots, and two gleaming white stripes on each sleeve, above which was the envied 'flaming A' that told the world I was a fully trained Ammunition Examiner in the Royal Army Ordnance Corps. I think Mum knew that her bundle of rags was going to turn out fine.

Spending every spare moment of the last term of my first

year at Chester with Phyllis helped me deal with the blow of losing my mother. I was a busy, ambitious young man, eager to get on with my own life, but stored-away shocks always surface in some way – since watching the ravaging effects of my mother's illness every problem in my life has gone straight to my stomach.

Phyllis started teaching a year before me, taking up a post as girls' physical education teacher at a secondary school at Wem in Salop. We had already decided to get married as soon as I qualified. There were teaching jobs by the ton then, you could go and get one almost anywhere you fancied, so we planned to work locally and live with Dad in his terraced house for the first term, while we saved up a deposit for a place of our own. I was happy to start work in Accrington because I felt safe there and Phyllis could get a job at the nearby Woodnook Secondary School. We both applied for and got the jobs we wanted, she at Woodnook and I at Hyndburn Park Secondary school, but before we took up our posts, I had to pass my exams and we had to fit in the wedding.

We had to be practical because suddenly we realized that the great wide world was out there and we wanted our place in it. Phyllis was incredibly stoical about it all and a wedding seemed like a necessary formality to enable us to get on with it. But the other necessary formality – my meeting with the approval of Phyllis's parents – was by no means easily passed over and I was not at all stoical about the prospect of handling what was to turn out to be a delicate situation.

I had to face a very protective mother and father, both of whom were determined that their number-one daughter should not be wasted on this bespectacled upstart. After all Phyllis had been to college and was a qualified schoolteacher with a promising future. Why should this northern male enter the arena and threaten all they had hoped for their daughter? In the late 50s parents who envisaged careers before marriage and children for their daughters were a rare breed – in fact, well ahead of their time. The strength of their feelings on this matter was repeatedly made clear to me.

From the minute I sat down at the tea table of Mr and Mrs Owen, I felt there was nothing I could do, say, eat or drink that would meet with their approval. They were polite but chilly and obviously determined to be unimpressed by their daughter's beau.

'Would you like another sandwich, James?' (The least you could do is eat more, after all we are butchers.)

'Some more tea?' (You're obviously not good enough for our daughter, but we're still polite enough to force you to drink the last cup. Then you can go.)

Phyllis was the peace ambassadress at all times and encouraged the adversaries to meet for Sunday tea as often as could not be reasonably avoided. It was easy for me to travel down from Chester for the weekend, but it was costly as I had to spend two nights in a hotel, since Mr and Mrs Owen refused to let me sleep under the same roof as their daughter.

Mr Owen made his opposition to me abundantly clear, and I wrote to him, saying, 'Your efforts to make it difficult for me to see Phyllis are a waste of time. There is nothing you can do to stop me.' My letter was bristling with anger and insults, but we grudgingly declared a truce.

'It is my intention to marry your daughter, Mr Owen,' I braved one Sunday after a few too many cups of tea. 'And it really would be nicer for Phyllis if we got married with your approval.'

Mr Owen smiled resignedly and said, 'Yes, of course. Hadn't you better propose then?'

So I had to get down on one knee in the butcher's lounge and propose to Phyllis in front of her father. She giggled, then accepted with a sweetly serious face, and from then on I didn't have to go round for tea quite as often. When I did, it was much less of an ordeal and I was able to enjoy the tea and sandwiches.

My student vacations turned back the wheel of time to Nori

Brickworks in Accrington, where I found a summer job through a contact of my father's. I think Dad liked the idea of my doing a stint at the brickworks.

When I was a seven-year-old everything about Dad's place of work had seemed impressively enormous. Working there as a student I was less in awe of the scale of the buildings and more aware of the heat and dust.

The kilns were a series of chambers arranged in an oval, each about twelve feet square and ten feet high. The bricks were made of clay from a nearby quarry and were either extruded or pressed to give them form, then dried to some degree in a huge drying room in preparation for final firing at a temperature of over a thousand degrees centigrade. At the pre-firing stage the bricks were called 'green'.

The setter's job was to set the 'green' bricks in the kiln, which involved carefully stacking the bricks in such a way as to allow the ever-moving fire to pass among the stacks evenly, ensuring smooth firing. When he had filled the kiln with green bricks, the setter would move on to the next kiln while the arched entrance to the kiln he had just filled was bricked up and rendered, thereby sealing the kiln. At intervals he would go up into the roof space above the kilns, where viewing holes enabled him to look down and watch the progress of the fire.

If the gaps between the bricks were too small, the bricks would fuse; if the fire came in too fast the bricks might fall over and you could lose a whole stack – catastrophe! The terracotta mouldings – of which my Dad was always so proud – were particularly temperamental and the placement of these very expensive creations was critical.

It was only through working at the brickworks, with all its attendant hazards, that I began to realize how hard Dad had worked to keep our ship afloat and how skilled he must have been, not only to become a setter but ultimately to be made foreman of the whole shebang. As foreman he had been manager of an unstoppable fire. What a job!

There was no room for lame ducks or passengers at the

brickworks in the 50s, because efficient teamwork was crucial to every aspect of the process. Reliance on your workmates was an integral part of the working day. From emptying the kilns ahead of the fire, to refilling them, to the loading of the lorries in order and on time – from quarry to factory gates, every stage of brickmaking involved the cooperation of a team. The tempo of work was dictated by the roaring fire; without friendly and reliable workmates it would have been hell on earth.

As a student I had the relatively easy job of moving the bricks out of the kilns after they had been fired. Emptying a kiln of five thousand fired bricks, each weighing eight pounds (two pounds less than in their green state) and having to wheel forty-eight of them at a time on a metal-wheeled barrow over a nine-inch-wide plank across the railway sidings demanded a different kind of concentration and agility from that I was used to as a trainee teacher. You couldn't stop because you were being chased by the fire.

Student workers are always fair game for factory pranks and the regulars kept me on my mettle by putting up dodgy planks so I'd topple over with the barrow now and again. The lovely thing about it was that the regular workers were pleased to have the students there and kept us in our place, back on planet earth. They took great pride in being far more worldly wise than we sharp alecs and made us constantly aware that life was about practicalities, coming to terms with what you have and not getting a book out and reading about it. I think that's been one of the attitudes that has remained with me – what's happening to you is under your feet, it ain't up in the sky. All there is up there these days is a lot of obsolete ironmongery and the odd monkey with information for the retrieval of.

'Oh, excuse me, don't come the academic here, young Whittaker. Pick up your bread, I've just nailed it to the floor next to your mug. Oh dear, is that nailed down too?' They pulled our legs because they knew we were kicking off to dance higher, but it was affectionately done and there was nothing nasty or vindictive about these pranks.

Another part of my job was helping to load the lorries by hand, wearing hand-leathers and throwing the bricks two at a time along a human chain from stack to lorry. Failing to catch the bricks precisely meant painfully nipped fingers, which motivated a very precise catching action. It was always reassuring if the man throwing the bricks to you was a friend. An enemy could give you a very uncomfortable time during the loading of a lorry by ensuring that the two bricks arrived in your hands not quite in unison. If the thrower had a real grudge against you, one of the two bricks coming towards you could be spinning. There were some very good fielders in the cricket teams of East Lancashire who were thoroughly coached, not on the green playing fields of Eton but in the loading bays of the Accrington Brick & Tile Company, deftly catching two eight-pound razor-edged projectiles on a speedy and regular basis!

In whichever part of the brickworks you worked, you were coated in dust. Nowhere in the process could you wear a white shirt with impunity for more than thirty seconds. There was grey-green dust, there was soot from the fire, and there was red dust and grit from the finished bricks.

Quite a few of my workmates were absolute nutters. There was Frannie Willesey who couldn't swear in one word. He couldn't just say 'blooming thing', he had to say 'bloody, swining, looning, damn, effing thing!' He seemed to have a little competition going with himself to see what was the longest list of expletives he could let out without taking a breath when something went wrong. Then there was a Methodist lay preacher – a brave one to work in the brick-works – who never swore. Even when his head was cut open by a flying brick when the loading line got out of kilter, he just said, 'Oh, blinking 'eck!' He went on catching and throwing the bricks whilst dabbing the blood from his forehead with a dusty handkerchief. His coordination was tested to its limits. I hope his wife had a Fisher automatic washing machine!

★

I passed my Certificate of Education exams (they didn't fail many people in those days either) and went to work another summer at the brickworks, saving my £7 a week wages towards our August wedding. I was already the proud owner of my first car, a blue 1955 Ford Prefect, registration PLW 714, which Dad had bought me for a handsome £400. In the summer of 1959 the boys at the brickworks made sure we got four hours' overtime for three nights to give me a bit extra for our honeymoon in Bispham.

My dad never met Mr and Mrs Owen until our wedding day, which was a trial for him because he had to stay over and share the bathroom. The day before our wedding, I arrived at the Owen residence in Oswestry to find Phyllis in the state of mind she usually assumes before an important event. She had decided to do something practical and was engrossed in painting the front of her parents' Victorian semi-detached house, three and a half storeys high. Phyllis looked very small indeed some thirty-five feet away at the top of a ladder.

'Come down, oh love divine,' I shouted. 'It makes me nervous watching you up there.'

Phyllis waved back. 'Don't worry. I'll be finished in good time to get into my dress.'

She was and she looked radiant. So did the paintwork on the upstairs windows.

10

Climbing the Chalk Face

When we newlyweds moved into the two-bedroomed terrace house on Harrington Street with Dad, he moved into his spare bedroom – made considerably bigger by taking out a chair – so Phyllis and I could have the double room at the front of the house. As I put on my suit for my first September day as a qualified classroom teacher I felt as if my life had come a full and rewarding circle round a cricket boundary, for our room offered an uplifting autumn view of the allotments and the opposite side of Enfield cricket ground from the one I'd grown up with at the old house in Dill Hall Lane. We also got the use of a flock mattress.

Slumped defiantly across the iron-framed bed, that mattress was like a nocturnal amoeba. You climbed into it, you didn't lie on it, and so became engulfed by an amorphous mass that absorbed all life as we know it. Any healthy urge to search for another human form in the bed was discouraged by the prospect of the climb over the mountainous ridge separating any two parties. This feat demanded so much energy that by the time the object of desire was reached, fatigue impaired performance. Suffice to say, there is a lot of truth in the story of the couple who bought their first interior sprung mattress to replace the flock one, but had to take it back to the shop with the embarrassed explanation, 'It's too fast for us!'

However, the amoebic nights were the least of our newly-wed concerns. Life at Dad's house was no picnic, in fact a pleasant evening spent next to the heater upstairs on a double decker bus was infinitely preferable to an evening at home. I was ungrateful and Dad was sullen. He had progressed through the strong and silent phase of his life to become an unrivalled expert at complete non-communication. Sometimes it became so bad that after we got off a bus Phyllis and I would splash out on a snack at Len's café on Market Street rather than go home before bedtime. Phyllis was much more patient with my dad than I was, and we knew that this was a one-term arrangement only. Our sights were firmly set on getting on with our teaching careers and saving for a home of our own by the end of the year.

The St James's annexe of Hyndburn Park Secondary School was a dark forbidding building near the centre of Accrington, with four classes of just over forty children each and a playground the size of a bus shelter. All four classes in the annexe worked in one large Victorian room divided by sliding partitions, so if a child in one classroom sneezed, a child in the next classroom took out his handkerchief. But I couldn't wait to get in there; I knew I was good and I was eager to get on with my career.

Anyway compared to the trials of living in the same house as Dad, teaching forty-four eleven-year-olds at Hyndburn Park was a leisure activity. I was made form master of 1D, a good class and smashing by the time I'd finished with them. At first I felt a little bit miffed about getting the bottom stream, because I thought it was meant as a reflection of my abilities. I had been given the class because I was academically the least qualified teacher in the year group, but I soon came to realize that didn't matter a toss. It was more important to be a teacher with 1D than with the top stream; the highfliers were going to achieve despite their teacher, whereas my class really needed me.

I enjoyed teaching them for all kinds of reasons, not least because I was doing the job my father had always wanted me to do, and 1D made my first year a great success. Having been in primary school classes along with forty-five or so other children who soaked up the primary school teacher's time, a lot of the children could hardly write. The intellectual minnows hadn't had the strength or personality to grab attention. So their heads were down when they came to me. Whatever else I did I wanted to get them to produce something they could take home and say, 'Hey, look what I've done!' They all made progress, particularly a young man called Richardson – I remember spending hours with him with reading. We both knew he was going to make it – and he did.

My spell with Sergeant Shelton in National Service meant that discipline came as second nature and the way my class was behaving told me I was getting it right. I could watch how they conducted themselves in the playground and the way they spoke to each other. I was giving my class homework when some of them did well to find their way home, never mind do homework when they got there.

I've heard from Richardson and from many others from that class since then and, touch wood, not one of them has come up to me and said, 'I didn't like you.' And I can assure you there were times in that classroom at St James's annexe when they despised me, they thought I was a horrible fiend.

I spent weeks, twenty minutes every morning teaching italic handwriting, a style which some now regard as intruding on individual development. The class hated it for the first few days, then they got to like it and took pride in their work. If you are teaching practical skills to a large number of people, it's a case of let's do this together. In the army the quickest way to get thirty men from A to B is to march them in line, in step and in control. Substitute thirty men for thirty pupils: more can be achieved if the teacher doesn't allow pupils to run off on a different route or straggle behind the rest of the class. Put everyone in the middle where they can be supported by their classmates; it's not a race and we'll all get there together, with more time to get on with the next stage.

There were distinct shades of Sergeant Shelton in my class-room manner.

Although many educationalists might wave their research papers in despair at these philosophies in the classroom, I found that a lot of the things I learned in the army are reflected in basic principles of classroom management and organization. Anyone who really believes that a teacher can walk into a classroom, not be in total control and still educate ought to go back to school to see how it feels as a pupil sitting on a ship with no captain. If this implies introducing the word 'fear' into the educative process, then so be it. Never let the teacher be afraid of imposing his will in his own way, assuming quite rightly that they are all caring professionals.

All the teachers I worked with at Hyndburn Park cared about the children. Mr Gidman, the head of the annexe, was a very kind, caring man who worried about his job. I never worried about mine. I didn't spend much time in the staff-room either – at morning playtime I would sometimes run off across the road and get oatcake biscuits in an attempt to perk up the tea break, then I'd walk back out of the staffroom almost as soon as the packet was opened, because I never really treated the staffroom as a place of rest and retreat. I don't think I was an easy member of staff to handle because I wished to make my presence felt and I did so by wanting to show off the children I was teaching. I wanted my class to be the best and I wanted everyone to know about it, so I was probably over self-confident and a pain in the neck, but at least I made sure I enjoyed my work. I wanted to make a name for myself and, as I had only the minimum teaching qualifications, no A-levels or degree, I was compensating by doing the extra-curricular activities, and getting attention by being outrageous. The only way I was going to progress was by being noticed for my feats of achievement rather than what was on my curriculum vitae.

In the autumn term I started as I meant to go on. I never stopped. Most evenings I ran after-school activities, usually games or gymnastics, and I had a Saturday morning football team. I also persuaded some of the parents to buy trumpets so we could set up a junior band to support Bill Nelson, a great guy who ran the brass band in the main school.

As an all-singing, all-dancing young probationary teacher, determined to make a name for himself in the world of education, I was probably perceived as a right little smartie! I once read an article by a famous Canadian businessman who wrote, 'Let us not be put off by feasibility. It will compromise us soon enough. Let us look at what can be achieved and be inspired by what we see.' That was my attitude and it rubbed off on the kids.

I was determined to get 1D to be the best class in the annexe, which I think they were by the end of the year – and not just in my eyes – not academically but as human beings, young people with self-esteem who felt just as good as any other child in the building. My class were proud to be in 1D. They were the ones with their heads held high, shiny faces, clean nails and teeth and shoes.

Sustained by forgettable lunches of beige cabbage from shiny canteen tins, I made the most of my evenings, initially to avoid spending them at home with Dad. When I became the nucleus of the Young Teachers' Association my interest in things theatrical quickly spurred me on to organize an amateur theatre group which put on a series of the Whitehall farces. The first was *See How They Run* with yours truly getting the funniest role. I thought if Brian Rix could do it, so could I.

At the same time I was working at a bottle factory a couple of evenings a week and saving every penny. It was lucky for me that Phyllis was teaching PE at Woodnook Secondary School, because she was involved in extra-curricular activities too. Otherwise she might have accused me of desertion during our first year of marriage. The only evenings she got home before me were those when I was out earning a bit extra at the bottle factory.

I couldn't have done so much without Phyllis. We were

batting together and determined to have a good innings. To buy a house in the new year we had to save £180 for the deposit, plus an extra seven pounds down because we had set our sights on a Baxi fire for an extra bit of glow. Our combined earnings for a month as schoolteachers was £80, so the deposit took a lot of earning and our contribution to Dad's housekeeping was nil. I don't think I showed much gratitude.

By the time I crept into bed each night I was shattered, but I was very young and had a lot of energy. Phyllis was with me all the way. We had shared objectives; we knew where we wanted to go and I was determined to get us off the bottom. Children didn't come into the frame at all at this stage.

Number 53 Queen Elizabeth Crescent, Accrington welcomed us with open windows as we fled from the flock mattress in January 1960. Our new bedroom suite cost £65, a wedding present from Phyllis's parents, and we borrowed £200 from the bank to get an Axminster carpet and a moquette three-piece suite. That was it – a roof over our heads and every incoming penny accounted for.

We were clearing about £8 a week each and if the grocery bill for the month was more than £6 we'd have an inquest. The week before payday would often find us popping over for a coffee at friends' houses and hoping and hinting that the cheese and biscuits would come out before we left. Phyllis always says I was funnier in those days than I am now. I was certainly hungrier and no doubt the sight of a cheese and tomato roll would improve my performance. Entertaining people was becoming a part of my life. At least people were laughing too much to notice whether I ate more than my fair share of cream crackers.

Phyllis was in her second year as a PE teacher when I was doing my first year, but at her new school she was quite shy and insecure. She came from a very traditional family and was still finding her wings. I never came home to domestic upheaval. She was the bedrock. Apart from being very clever, she is also a very manipulative lady and she could handle me. If I was going very wrong or over the top in some way she would move the tiller without my knowing, alter direction slightly, nudge me on course.

For my second year of teaching I got a tiled hall and a brass band and went from teaching general subjects back to my specialisms of maths and PE. I had been after a job in the main school and got it when Bill Nelson left. Now I had a proper gym area I could spend more time on what I was best at and keep my eyes and ears open for a move to head of a PE department. Euan Davis, the area's PE inspector, let me do a few demonstration lessons to make myself known.

I was also very happy to take over the school band from Bill Nelson, and struggled through by keeping one page ahead of the children in the tutor book. I'd done a little band-leading down at St James's annexe and cajoled mums and dads into buying instruments.

Al fresco band practice was one of my favourite extra-curricular activities. As there was no question of funds for a lawn outside our house in Queen Elizabeth Crescent, the idle patch of earth offered an ideal spot to gather as many children as I could muster and help them make a lot of noise. There would often be six or seven kids at a time – they all brought their own instruments along to our untilled plot, found a comfortable stone to sit on, and there we used to practise pieces such as *Allegro Spiritoso* and *John Brown's Body*. The band perfected a rousing interpretation of the latter which was particularly well received at parents' evenings.

In my second year of teaching I was able to make a little extra money from selling petrol at Hillock Vale garage in Accrington (part of the Henry Gilbraith group) and it was there that I made the acquaintance of Bill and Elsie Derbyshire. Bill was very good company, a great man to relax with, and it was during this era that I gave up drinking spirits. Fortunately for me, it was well before I could afford to buy them. It happened after a long night on the whisky with Bill.

Elsie had gone off to Chorley with Phyllis to see a fashion show, and Bill and I settled down for a night in with a bottle of scotch. I'd never drunk much whisky before, but it seemed to go down nicely and between the two of us we emptied the bottle. What a marvellous example of being in the right place at the right time in the right company . . . drinking the wrong substance. I was in a terrible state. I could hardly stand by ten o'clock, when, having suddenly decided that I had to see Phyllis, I lurched out of the house into the night to call for her.

'Phyllis! Phyllis! Come inside please! Come back Phee-llee-ees!' I screeched as if she were in the back garden. When she didn't come I just kept on shouting, never considering that my voice might not travel the thirty or so miles to Chorley and she might not hear me even if all the neighbours could. I couldn't understand why Phyllis wasn't there when I felt so ill.

When Phyllis and Elsie did come back they brought fish and chips for supper and I was ecstatically pleased to see them. Such was my deep delight at the vision of my long-lost wife offering me a plate of cod and chips that I decided to celebrate by flinging them into the air. In my scotched mind they resembled fireworks. One for the pelmet, one for each picture frame, a spray for the hearth, one for each corner of the ceiling. As I remember, the light fitting appeared to be particularly deserving of fatty adornment but, try as I might, I couldn't get one chip to lodge neatly next to each light bulb.

When I refused to stop sharing my chips with the fixtures and fittings, Phyllis suggested I go into another room to calm down and she says I followed her on all fours (by now the only position in which I could cover any ground without falling over), flinging food in my wake. I have no memory of what happened next, but was told that I was bundled upstairs and locked in the bathroom, from where I begged, 'Please let me out, the curtains need more chips.'

I do remember the physical and mental agony of the next

Playing *Cherry Pink* on *The Wheeltappers and Shunters*, 1976. The lady next
to me was disrobing in sympathy.

Phyllis showing her deep appreciation of my great musical talent.
(Harold Holborn)

My only claim to real academic fame, at the Oxford Union, 1992.

Home sweet home!

day, when my lunatic actions of the previous night were explained to me and my head seemed as though it belonged to someone else. I felt so ill that the smell of whisky still makes me feel queasy. Since that day I have not touched scotch and would never do so even for large amounts of money. Anything that can persuade your brain that a chip is a Golden Rain firework has got to be dangerous. I do my best to avoid holding a barside conversation with scotch drinkers, as even just the smell reminds me of the terrible aftermath of that night with Bill Derbyshire. Of course, it was the best thing that could have happened to me because I've never got into the habit of drinking spirits and I've seen so many of my contemporaries get wrecked with them. I just drink bitter – for Europe. Fortunately I'd always been a beer man and bitter has helped me in my work, or rather after my work.

When a department head vacancy came up in 1961 at St Ambrose's Roman Catholic Secondary School in Raw-tenstall, I applied. The interview board's first choice candidate turned down the job, so they offered it to me. Being second choice didn't matter an iota; it was another case of being in the right place at the right time – hello St Ambrose of Rawtenstall and £100 rise, a responsibility payment and the first step in the climb up the ladder of education.

At that time it was still easy to be confident about promotion because there were so many jobs around that teachers could pick and choose. The changes in education that were in the air in the 60s made it an exciting time for the teaching profession. Training colleges instilled the idea of keeping the best of the old and experimenting with the best of the new, but experimentation hadn't yet taken over and attracted critical press.

My new headmaster at St Ambrose's was a very modern, idealistic man with severe asthma. Jim Howard's enthusiasms were firmly directed into devising new school record charts to monitor ability levels. (He would have loved the flood of standardized yellow profile cards that the government has recently unleashed to brighten up staffrooms all over the nation – thank goodness somebody somewhere still has to sit the pupils down and actually teach them where Africa is.) Jim Howard and I worked from opposite ends of the process – I eyeballed the fat boys and said, 'Come on, Johnnie, you can get over that box' and Jim chased me to put a tick on Johnnie's chart. The headmaster didn't get in my way, though; in fact I hardly saw him.

Rawtenstall is only about seven miles from Accrington and I changed our car for commuting. The Ford Prefect was replaced by an Austin A40, registration number UUJ 876. Isn't it funny remembering all the registration numbers? I suppose it's because I've always had a love of cars and they have been important to me in my work too. In the early 60s I drove to as many evening courses and demonstration lessons at different schools as I could fit into a week. PE teachers had to keep in tune with the trends or get sent out to pasture with the second eleven, and the fast route to the front line involved catching the eye of Mr Percy Jones, the area PE organizer whose manicured finger was firmly on the pulse of progress and whose voice counted at County Hall.

St Ambrose and I were planning my next move and Percy was to be a central figure in my escape plot. I hope by this stage you're not forming the impression that I'm a conniving devious monomaniac who will aim for promotion and acquire it at any cost. That is far from the truth, although having read this back to myself, I am beginning to think I could well have been verging on the fanatical at times in my efforts to progress. Read the next chapter; things may well become more leisurely.

11

Billington, My Broadway

A fussy Welshman whose trousers never wrinkled and whose sense of humour lay deep in a distant green valley, Percy Jones was a prolific writer of pamphlets that helped put Lancashire in the spotlight in the field of educational gymnastics. Percy's pride and joy was a film made by a Haslingden teacher called Jim Taylor. The Haslingden Film, as it was known, was the bee's knees. Everyone referred to it and revered it; inspired by it I decided it was my turn.

I'd arrived at St Ambrose's determined to make a filmic contribution to education that would lift me higher than the highest heights of Haslingden. I set about those boys who had never done educational gymnastics before. St Ambrose was a new Roman Catholic school which had amalgamated five or six other smaller RC secondary schools so the pupils had had access to a large gymnasium for only a year or so. I worked hard with them, put them in a gymnastic greenhouse. After a few weeks I picked out the best three classes and trained them up like circus performers to give us a highly polished educational gymnastics lesson.

It seemed almost stage-managed, but I had to get Percy to notice my work so that he would help me to go on to make the next educational gymnastics film to come out of Lancashire.

I spent so much time trying to carve a niche for myself in the progress of educational gymnastics that soccer and other sports on the curriculum didn't get much attention. I also put on a parents' evening where I did a gymnastics exhibition with all the tricks, not dissimilar from army demonstrations for parents. It was just about making a mark for myself really and this I did to some extent at the expense of the boys all-round PE, but the self-satisfaction and success they got from being the exhibition classes more than compensated for the fact that they didn't get perhaps quite as much time playing football and cricket. I didn't question in my own mind the arena I'd chosen, but came to terms with the route I took.

'I'm destined to make that film, Phyllis,' I said to her one night on the moquette.

'St Ambrose's Gymnasium Productions?'

'Not yet, not at St Ambrose's. First I've got to get my classes performing like clockwork, then get Percy Jones to bring people to watch my lessons, then make a film with him and become a guru of Lancashire gymnastics. It's good for the boys and it's also the fashion ... I want to make an impression in my subject while it's still hot, so people will say, "Have you seen the Whittaker film?" I'll be a pioneer of progress ...'

'Yes, Jim, that sounds good. And you won't even have to have a screen test,' said Phyllis, having quietly checked the tiller to make sure I was sailing a good course.

Percy Jones was my mentor in Rawtenstall. I was to become his number one man. When I first asked him to come and see one of my classes that I'd got ready for a demonstration, he sounded surprised.

'You've only been there three months. I know you've done some good work, but you're not trained in PE, are you?'

'Well, I didn't go to Carnegie or Loughborough,' I had to admit. 'But I am head of the PE department. I've got a great class here and I think you'll enjoy seeing what we're doing.'

'I'll come along and see how it's going,' said Percy, sounding more wary than fired with enthusiasm.

He came to St Ambrose's, and returned the following week with a group of students from Carnegie College in Leeds to see my teaching methods. I had been insufficiently qualified to apply for a place on the teacher training course at Carnegie, but now I was showing them the business – sequence work on the mats, rolling movements, variations of speed, height, stretches, taking body weight on different parts. And the children loved it. They were well aware of how much progress they had made in three months, even if I hadn't got round to marking up all their record cards yet. The demonstration lesson was an overall picture of achievement on their part and on mine. I felt I had achieved something important – in my way I was their Miss Pilkington. Soon observers were coming in every week to watch lessons, sometimes rows of dark blue Carnegie blazers with the discus badge, sometimes the Loughborough Adonis. I was centre stage and loving every minute.

When Carnegie students come all the way from Leeds to Lancashire to see you, you know you're on the gravy train. Anyone brave enough to cross the red/white rose border has got to be coming to see something worthwhile.

Although I tried to avoid discussing my work in the pub, Phyllis got her ear bent quite a lot, because I was always talking about gymnastics. I decided to write pamphlets with a few of my own buzzwords thrown in. 'How does this sound, Phyllis . . . Having established objectives, condition the exercise by imposing limitations . . .'

I was flattered to notice some of my words turning up in Percy's pamphlets.

In my second term at Rawtenstall, St Ambrose helped us to move house – to 428 Burnley Road in Accrington – but I was moving fast and within eighteen months we had yet another address, as St Augustine stepped in with a new job that took Phyllis and me to 12 Beaver Close in Blackburn and new jobs that let us work back to back in two massive gymnasiums with £150 pay rises to play with in the pantry.

St Augustine's Roman Catholic School in Billington was a peach – two of the biggest gymnasiums in the district, four trampettes, ten acres of playing fields, twelve tennis courts, three soccer pitches, and new equipment on demand. Phyllis and I were panting for Billington when both boys' and girls' PE posts fell vacant. In our book these were the best jobs in Lancashire.

My application was backed by Percy, who also happened to ask, 'Why doesn't Phyllis apply for the girls' post?'

'Oh, what a nice idea,' said Phyllis, and her plimsolls started to twinkle.

Perhaps we should never have got the jobs. But the full power of Percy was behind us because he fancied a male and female flagship for gymnastics. And the headmaster, Mr Worthington, was all for it because he had wanted his own wife on the staff and the governors had rejected the idea of a husband and wife team. Worthington wanted us as a lever, so we both got the jobs. It wasn't exactly fixed but the order in the promotion queue was given a severe looking at. We went out to celebrate that night at our local, the Red House, delighted that we were both on the way.

Children still hadn't featured on our horizons, we were just delighted that we seemed to be making a success of our lives and we started to be able to afford things like bread and tea – no, seriously, we started to enjoy quite a nice lifestyle. The car got a bit better; I got a Vauxhall VX490, registration BMX 256A and a real beauty. We were looking forward to doing full justice to the gigantic gymnasiums that awaited. And I have to say in hindsight that we did do that.

We made St Augustine's RC School in Billington the mecca for gymnastics in the county. I put up a wall display in the entrance hall, with photographs and arrows going off at every angle, so that as soon as you walked into the school you knew it was a gymnastics showcase. I had three or four classes of untouchable gymnasts who soon got used to giving demonstrations almost weekly to teachers and trainee teachers from all over the county and beyond. The boys would come in with sparkling eyes and straight backs, and it was sheer showbiz. We put on an immaculate display, a perfectly timed cabaret, with back somersaults, head and shoulder springs.

I had the fattest boys doing rolls, cartwheels and somersaults and acting as buttresses for the more lithe flippers. Percy was pleased. He wrote a book using photographs from the displays and, as I'd promised Phyllis, we made a film. The Billington film is still shown to trainee teachers in the 1990s.

Having won the boys' trust because I was a motivator, I could get them to reach that extra six inches, I could get that extra little bit of effort out of them that made them special. They twinkled with star quality in the film.

One day I was taking 3C, who are featured on the film, and I had an unforgettable conversation with a pupil called Jackson, who was hanging upside down on the wall bars at the time.

'Where can you go from there?' I asked him.

'Well, I could let go with one arm and make an asymmetric shape on the bars, sir,' came his enthusiastic reply.

'Good. Now could you let go with the other arm?'

No sooner had I got out the words than he did let go and, of course, landed straight on his head. Thankfully he bounced and was unharmed, so I said, 'Hey, well, you've got to think as well, Jackson . . .'

Hanging on a nail at the back of my office door for all to see was an old plimsoll named Horace. If someone forgot their kit they got three Horaces. The plimsoll hurt – there would have been no point in using it if it didn't hurt but it didn't do any damage. Of course, I couldn't say that if I were still in the teaching profession or I'd probably be arrested. It sounds sadistic now, but so do the current incidences of pupils attacking staff. The very presence of Horace ensured it needed to be used very rarely indeed.

Teachers are not in the business of hurting children, but in the business of making them aware members of society who respect the law of the school and the law of the land – in other words it's horses for courses. In an ideal world there would be no need for a punishment system; Horace could be superglued to the door. But, as we all know, the ideal world ain't out there. As it was, Horace the plimsoll often got very dusty at Billington, showing that it was doing its job. The plimsoll was treated with humorous respect and with most of the boys it was unnecessary.

At the beginning of one Friday afternoon lesson Terry Dewhurst, the captain of the first soccer team, came to the pitch carrying Horace. I couldn't believe he'd forgotten his kit because he lived for soccer and the team had a big game coming up.

'I'll have to have Horace today, sir', said Terry. 'I think I've had too much dinner. It was fish and chips and steamed pudding and custard.'

The only answer to that was 'Go and hang up Horace and come and watch.'

Phyllis's only problem with discipline was that she got passed on other teachers' problems. The headmaster believed in corporal punishment with the cane and delegated serious discipline of the girls to the senior mistress who delegated it to Phyllis, who was expected to punish girls on occasion for some misdeed that had happened hours earlier and which she hadn't witnessed. This used to destroy Phyllis because smacking a child at three o'clock in the afternoon for something she'd done wrong at eleven o'clock in the morning seems, to say the least, thoughtless and insensitive.

If a child is disruptive you have to deal with it instantly. My way has sometimes been a kick up the backside, to hurt not damage, corporal punishment doesn't enter into my vocabulary. You deal with a situation the best way you can and the very best way ensures that you don't have to do it often because it's effective. If you care enough about children, you are going to get it right. You're going to get it wrong the odd times, too.

The big difference today is that schoolteachers have so little going for them. A child can tell a teacher to eff off and the teacher can do precious little about it. The teaching profession is no longer the profession we knew. I'd like to see teachers get back on stage and be paid well for doing great work.

When I had a hundred trainee teachers watching me teach a gymnastics class, I loved every minute of it. I was only five years older than some of the students in the audience and I wanted to be the doyen, so I played to the stalls. The children and I all put on our best performances. I flaunted my control of the classes and the children flaunted their gymnastic skills. My approach to career enhancement was unashamedly theatrical. If you've got it, flaunt it, and if you can't give the pupils something to flaunt, you shouldn't be a teacher.

After a rewarding performance in the gymnasium at Billington nothing pleased me more than an evening at the Ace of Spades club in Whalley, one of my favourite haunts. Mike Shaun was compère and every week introduced cabaret acts, often star names such as Max Wall and Guy Mitchell. The club also had a casino, so I presumed that the money lost by gamblers paid for the star names. I was intrigued by Mike Shaun's performance. He was a very able compère and wore an impressive bronze mohair suit. I found that I was thinking more and more about being up there on stage myself.

The Ace of Spades offered a more intimate view of showbusiness than when I'd seen Doddy in the theatres and all the acts on stage in Blackpool. In the cabaret clubs you really could smell the greasepaint. The venues were smaller and the audience nearly always much closer to the performer, in a far more informal setting. Without the proscenium arch the almost invisible barrier between performer and audience vanished. It was far better for the audience because they could see the artistes in much greater detail; by the same rule the proximity of the audience to the performer, I was shortly to learn, could be quite unnerving. It's the whites-of-the-eyes syndrome.

I'm not sure a performer likes to see the whites of the eyes of the audience – after all, there are invariably far more of them than him. This was a greater problem for the traditional theatre performer than the newer breed of cabaret artiste. In fact, it's quite a luxury for a cabaret artiste to work in a theatre with no distractions like drink, bingo, arrival of pies or death of club secretary. However, as I watched the cabaret in the Ace of Spades and it gradually became clear to me how much I wanted to be part of the action, I knew that my starting place would involve many pie suppers and bingo games.

I realized then that the way to the nightclub scene was through the working men's clubs, and that if I was to make any progress as a performer it had to be done parallel to my work as a teacher, as at this time I still believed that my future lay in the education system. I thought I could have the best of both worlds for a time. I was already enjoying the thrill of performing in front of students of physical education when, quite by chance, I discovered another area where I could perform in front of the public and possibly get paid for doing it.

12

Moving into Mohair

One Sunday lunchtime in 1964 I found myself at the Regent Hotel in Blackburn, watching a stand-up comedian whom I found mediocre. The teachers at Billington had laughed more than this at my jokes in the staffroom.

'I can do better than him,' I said to Phyllis, and the next thing I knew I was up there standing at the microphone. The manager of the Regent had heard my smug comment and had promptly gone up on stage to announce me as the next act. And thus I had fame thrust upon me in Penny Street, Blackburn.

As soon as I started to tell my first joke, a little voice in my head reminded me that I only knew three gags altogether, so I'd better not hurry. I made them last by drawing upon my very limited comedic resources. I didn't reach double figures in terms of minutes and certainly not in terms of laughs, but my performance was good enough to attract the attention of Bill Eckersley, one-time captain and right-back of Blackburn Rovers and England. Before I left the Regent he offered me a booking at Ewood Social Club and mentioned the figure of three pounds. I honestly thought that was a reasonable amount to pay to learn to be a comedian. Imagine my delight when I realized *he* was paying *me*.

At Ewood Social Club I got the bug. I tasted laughter which I had extracted from an audience deliberately and I

liked the feeling it gave me. My comedy learning curve ran
nearly vertically for the following twelve months, for I took
every opportunity to appear at every working men's club
within driving distance; Liberal, Labour, Conservative,
Catholic, Protestant, Bowling or Railwaymen's, I'd go anywhere I knew there was a microphone, music and people.

Encouraged by the fun and the fees, I developed an urgent
need for a shiny suit. I didn't want to be a cloth-cap comic.
I don't suit a cap. And the alternative was the mohair suit,
after Mike Shaun.

Cliff Walmsley's Gents Outfitters in Accrington revealed
to me exactly the suit I needed. It was grey mohair, single-
breasted, with tapered trousers, and had that certain sheen.
I had to have that suit. It was as sophisticated as the Ace of
Spades in Whalley. I would peer in the shop window with
the same feeling of longing that Tiny Tim felt when he gazed
at the biggest turkey in the world before Alistair Sim gave it
to him in the movie. Within a week desire overcame me and
I rashly marched into the shop to buy the suit. Fortunately
Mr Walmsley had two or three sizes in stock and both my
legs were the same length, so I got one that fitted well.

'This is going to be my stage suit,' I told Mr Walmsley,
trying to make him feel like Alistair Sim. 'I shall wear it
tonight at the Willow Mount Club, Accrington as I am
appearing in cabaret there.'

In fact, I was going to try and squeeze on stage for no fee
between the acts that were really booked there. As I put on
the suit, with a carefully chosen dark tie and a white button-
down collar, I knew that neither wild horses nor wild pie-
sellers would keep me from giving my new mohair its début.
I thought I cut quite a shimmering figure at the Willow
Mount Club. And you'll have to believe me, because all
photographs have been destroyed.

During this era, my mid-60s mohair phase, I was like
Gracie Fields, taking her harp to the party and hoping
someone would ask her to play. I wore my suit and hoped
someone would ask me to tell a joke. Every night I'd get

home from Billington school, Phyllis and I would decide whether to eat now or pie later, then I would jump into the suit and we'd take off to a club because Phyllis preferred the smoke-laden halls of working men's clubs to staying at home alone. I trusted her as my best critic. Evenings were something of a continuation of our working together in the same school during the day, except there was more to laugh at.

At one club in Blackburn my first two spots had gone very well, but before my third one Phyllis unwittingly bought tickets for the bingo game in the interval and won. Word went round the club in a flash that the turn's wife had won the bingo. Phyllis collected her one pound five shillings for a full house and I went on to stony silence.

Gradually I built up an act. My first jokes were typed out on little cards, and from there I progressed to writing clues on my wrists in biro – not a good idea in the heat of a Saturday night working men's club. Confusion and panic reigned when the ink ran and I looked at my wrist to see nothing more than smudges on my shirt cuff and my watch telling me how much time I had left to fill now that I had dried up completely.

Laughter now had a major role in my life, which I had to come to terms with. Was I doing it for me, for the audience or for the money? Certainly not for the money, because that was negligible. On reflection I believe I was doing it for myself at that time, for the buzz. As the years progressed I learned that there was more to making people laugh than just seeking out a buzz.

As the 60s progressed and my career in the teaching profession moved steadily forward as planned, I was also beginning to realize that within a part of me there was a full-time comedian trying to get out. But life as a stand-up comic was only a pencilled-in possibility, because this was also a time when career doors were flying open on all sides in the world of education, so I still felt that my future lay in teaching.

While happy to have made my mark in gymnastics, I was

aware that I wasn't an overall success as a PE teacher. If I hadn't been so obsessed with gym demonstrations I could probably have done a better job by spending more time on other sports and other aspects of education, but the compensation for the pupils was that we got a lot of achievers and the morale of the school rose considerably. When I had made the Billington film, pleased the crowds and been asked to give lectures as far away as Winchester, I was ready to move on to pastures new.

'You know, I like the smell of the lecture theatre,' I said to Phyllis on the moquette.

'Yes, you'll be wanting a lectureship next, I suppose?'

'Got it in one. It would be my chance of being a big fish in a little pond of physical education. To move that far up the ladder I will have to get a headship by the time I am thirty.'

'You'll have to go off and do another course then. Which one do you have in mind? As long as it's not a million miles away ...'

'How would you feel about Weybridge? It's not exactly Casablanca.'

'What's in Weybridge?'

'The Laban Dance Institute. I've started to introduce music and movement into the gym and it's going well. There's a lot of interest in the subject at the moment.'

Phyllis chuckled. 'Percy may never speak to you again.'

I thought Percy Jones was going to faint when he first heard the Beatles' *Penny Lane* playing in the gym. 'What's happened to the handstands, the somersaults and the floor sequences?' he asked in such undisguised horror that I wondered if he'd seen me in my off-duty mohair.

'Keep your creases in, Percy, the handstands and rolls and sequence work are still there but I'm moving on a bit here. I'm bringing in a element of creativity for the classes now, so I'm moving into some dance alongside the gymnastics.'

Percy's nostrils dilated, his eyes widened and seemed to

rest on my groin for a second, as if to confirm that I'd completely lost my manhood and was about to be measured up for a frock. *Penny Lane* was a trip too far for him. He'd been hinting that I should apply to take the advanced course at Carnegie College in Leeds, one of the most prestigious PE colleges in the country at the time, ranked with Lough-borough and St Luke's in Exeter. And here was his hot tip for college tutor, defiling the best gymnasium in the county with the Beatles and telling him, 'I've decided not to go for the place at Carnegie. I'd like a year's secondment to study dance at the Laban Institute in Weybridge.'

I got the secondment but Percy dropped me like a ton of bricks. If he had walked into one of the dance studios at the Laban Institute he would indeed have been a very unhappy man. Dance, as taught in the Laban Institute, was totally alien to all that Percy had done in terms of male gymnastics. To the old school of PE teachers dance and creative move-ment were verging on the effeminate – well, in the thick of it. You had to be very light on your feet. I chose to study dance because it was a fashionable trend, but I also believed it had a valid contribution to make in schools. I was confident in my leotard and leather pumps that dance was the way of the future and exactly the right thing to be studying in 1967.

For Percy, however, this was to be the end of what had been a very fruitful and productive friendship.

From now on I was choreographing my own career with no support whatsoever from Lancashire's Mr PE but with a little more help from working men's clubs, which brought in enough extra money to pay my train fares from Weybridge at weekends.

While Phyllis was lumbered with taking over a lot of my classes at Billington, I was living in a twelve-foot lemon caravan that I'd managed to park unobtrusively behind a little copse in the grounds of the Laban Institute. (Phyllis and I still have a caravan in our lives. It's parked at the end of the garden and she sends me down there when I'm being unbearable in the house or when I get into serious trouble for not eating my greens.)

The dance course was demanding. Students were rarely required to stand around being flowers opening in the sunshine or grass swaying in the breeze, as Percy had predicted. But there were even stranger things to learn. Although studying the aims of education through modern dance gave me a new perspective on physical education, some of the areas of study involving 'space harmony', the 'effort cube', the 'ico space model' and the 'dimensional cross' left me ungripped. I muddled through the course with a diagram here and a physical exhibition there.

Rudolf Laban was born in Bratislava in 1879 but his largest influence has been in the UK. After founding the Choreographic Institute in Würzburg, he moved to Berlin, fled to Addlestone in 1936 and then to Manchester, where he spent ten years consolidating his dance activities and theories with Lisa Ullman.

Laban allotted a symbol to each part of the body and the way it moves, providing his students with an extensive list of symbols to learn, as the difference between dance notation and music scoring is that there is an almost infinite number of moves that the human body can make. The Laban method of notation is one of the best known systems of recording dance steps, but I've never used it since.

However, I did move as much as I possibly could during the dance classes. I had to because my living quarters provided severe restrictions on movement of any kind. Fortunately I scraped through the exams, I think because I did a few good drawings.

With a new qualification under my belt, I was in line for a lectureship. I could do the educational gymnastics, the soccer, the swimming and, although I wasn't top of the range on qualifications, I also had a rare string to my bow because I was one of only about twenty male teachers in the country who had an advanced qualification in dance. So when I got an interview at a college of education in Essex, it was my big chance. And it was also the first time in my life I was well and truly stitched up.

I was selected out of 110 applicants for the final interview in Clacton along with one other guy who had a qualification in Dance and Drama. We were talking before the interview and, as I knew that my weak area was watersports, I laid my cards on the table and said, 'There's the estuary not far from here, so I suppose they'll be keen on canoeing and sailing. I haven't taught watersports, have you?'

'Erm, no I can't say I have,' he replied, fiddling with his socks.

'Why don't we both say we're intending to do a summer course in watersports so we'll be prepared for the autumn term, then we've got an even chance?'

The guy brightened visibly and agreed.

I felt quite confident about getting the job because this guy seemed so nervous and distracted that I thought he might fall off his chair or shred his socks before he was called to face the interviewing panel.

My interview went well. I'd met one of the interviewers at a summer school and he had also been to a lecture of mine and seen me teaching educational gymnastics, so he knew what I was about. At the end of the interview he said, 'Well, Jim, we've seen your film, we know your work, the only thing we need to talk to you about really is your watersports.'

I said, 'I've got the swimming certificate and taught swimming for six years, but I haven't done any other watersports so I intend to do the Physical Education Association's three-week course in Blackpool this summer. Then I won't be green when I come to you in October. And if you need me to do any more courses, I'll do those at the first opportunity.'

As it was everything had gone according to plan. I felt like big news and the interviewers were obviously impressed.

When I walked out of the room and saw the other guy hunched up nervously inside his suit, I was thinking, You poor little plonker, what a shame. I shouldn't bother going in to the interview room if I were you but never mind, go on and have a go. It will be good experience for you to follow hot property like me.

In my mind I had already secured the lectureship. I'd be so good at it my demonstration lectures would attract students from all over the globe and I might even become an inspector. This was my life's ambition coming true. I wanted to get up there where the action was and my ideas and philosophies would have some impact. I'd planned my entire upwardly mobile career path through Essex and had got round to wondering whether to wear leather patches on the elbows of a tweed jacket or stick with the body-building blazer as favoured by pernickety Percy by the time my rival emerged from his interview. Crushed, I thought.

'Everything go according to plan?' I asked him, still feeling a bit sorry for him but thinking at least I'd helped him over a little difficulty.

'Yes, fine thanks,' he murmured.

We both sat waiting. The drill was that all the candidates sit in the room after the interviews and one of the interviewing panel comes out and invites back in the man to whom they are going to offer the job.

After a while the senior lecturer came out and saw us sitting there and coolly invited the other chap in again. He'd got the blooming job. I'd been pipped at the post! I was ruined! Pride had come before the fall. I walked out near to tears.

'That guy knows me. He's seen my film. He knows I can communicate. He knows I'm a good teacher. Why did they choose that wet winge?' I asked myself over and over again. 'What has he got over me? I must have messed up on something very important to get to the final two out of 110 and then miss it ...' And as I was wailing inwardly the lecturer fell in step beside me.

'Jim, why didn't you say you could do watersports like the other guy did?'

'What!'

'We had to give the job to him because he's done a watersports course.'

Oh well, another one joins the old Youth Employment Officer from Padiham in my Obliterati file of minuscule minds.

Thanks to this particular Obliterati member I didn't become a lecturer, so I'll never know how I would have fared as an Essex Man, and at the time it was a difficult return north. Phyllis had given in her notice at Billington, as we'd planned, so it was time for a meeting on the moquette.

13

Habemus Papa

'Do you think southerners believe I'm not quite as bright as I might be because of my northern accent?' It was difficult giving up the idea of being a lecturer before I was thirty.

'How about aiming for Lancaster? That's north. We can both get jobs there, rent a flat in Morecambe and take it from there,' Phyllis suggested.

She knew I had some useful contacts for mohair evening work in Morecambe, so we identified our route forward and I found cause to be optimistic: 'I've seen a job advertised for a deputy head of a primary school. I think that's my avenue now, because dance is still very much in vogue as a modern educational trend, and I'm competing against people with four years' training in higher education. If I get to be a deputy head I can be a tasty little extra with the dance and drama, then become a head, and then maybe I can get a lectureship.'

'Of course you can,' said Phyllis.

So I applied to St Paul's Church of England Primary School in Caton near Lancaster and got an interview with a lovely headmaster called Cecil Wilkes and a gentle vicar named John Mullineaux. I was keen to step into the shoes of a very good deputy head, Jim Rogerson, who had just left the job. Jim was an excellent motivator with a superb command of the English language. He went on to work with children with learning difficulties and later wrote a television series called 'King Wilbur III' which I narrated on television in 1977.

Four applicants were shortlisted for the job in Caton. After my interview I sat and waited outside for seven months, maybe even nine, until the vicar came out and invited me back in. I knew I'd made it. I'd won. I was thirty-one and on my way. At that moment I felt sure I would be a headmaster by the time I was thirty-three.

'We'd like to offer you the job . . .'

'Thank you, thank you very much, vicar . . . I know I'm following a great act. What about a house?' I asked, and was helped towards a new address in Clougha Avenue, Halton, a convenient distance to drive to school and, as it happened, to a number of working men's clubs around Lancaster.

I entered the world of primary education as deputy head and found fresh inspiration working with a younger age group. We had a memorable success with a dance interpretation of the Easter story, performed in Caton Parish Church. *Luck Be A Lady Tonight* played when the Roman soldiers threw dice beneath the Cross as they gambled for Jesus's cloak. Some of the parents looked a little stunned at hearing jazz in church, but they sat up and paid attention; they loved it. The church pews were packed to capacity for three consecutive nights. Seats in no parts, probably for the first time since the church had been built.

'You'll know whether the performance has gone well if you get a certain little twinkling feeling in your stomach,' I told the excited cast before their first night. 'You'll know what I mean when you get it right.'

The children gave it their all. I'd seen them rehearse a hundred times, but even I was surprised at how moving the performance was. 'I've got it, sir, I've got that twinkle,' many of them said to me afterwards.

They got the 'twinkle' from two out of the three performances, and it was also to their credit when they felt that they hadn't given their best performance on the last night. I was, after all, reaping rich rewards from my course at the Laban Institute.

The local college of education, St Martin's, was aware that I had been a Laban pupil and sent me postgraduate students on teaching practice. Again I found myself orchestrating demonstration lessons to present to groups of trainee teachers. I think the children enjoyed them as much as I did.

The evenings saw me giving a rather different kind of demonstration – working semi-professionally in clubs. The daytime and evening skills overlapped to some extent, but my audience at school didn't laugh as much and didn't have pints of beer on their desks.

I didn't get much time to study the new wallpaper in Clougha Avenue, because Phyllis and I quickly got back into the old routine of jumping in the car after school and driving towards music and a microphone.

I tried to visit the Wilton Lounge at the Broadway Hotel in Morecambe every Thursday night, for the weekly appearance of the Jan Brezinka Big Band. Sometimes I would displace the very able Eddie Ferguson and thrust myself upon them as compère for part of the evening. They didn't seem to mind my introducing them as the Jan Brezinka Polish State Orchestra!

One of the leading lights of Jan Brezinka was Ray Robinson, a very good tenor/alto saxophone player. He and I struck up a friendship and we would chat together in the interval, admiring the two most prominent features of the Wilton Lounge which belonged to an attractive lady who sold pies on a tray. I'm sure she got the job because the pies remained hot for longer when carried close to her ample frame. She never actually served the pies herself. She couldn't see them, so we just took pies from under her human heated canopy, told her how many we'd taken and paid her accordingly.

After our ritualistic waiting for the pie lady, Ray and I would discuss music over her warming wares. When he expressed the desire to have his own band, we recruited one petrol tanker driver, Ernie Townson, as piano player; one primary school teacher (now headmaster), Mike Croft, who brought his double bass; and one professional musician, Noddy, who played the drums extremely well. With a fully formed band to take on the road, Ray and I then became the musical equivalent of double-glazing salesmen. We named our musical package the Ray Martin Sound (because the Ray Robinson Sound might have evoked the thud of a boxing glove) and hawked it around every available room on the west coast of Great Britain.

Eventually we struck gold at the Morecambe British Legion on Edward Street, a working men's club whose patrons were meant to be former soldiers and their families, but the club had a very liberal membership arrangement. They had always had an organist and a drummer to back the singer of the week, so it was our task to try to convince a committee meeting that the club needed a four-piece band and a compère for three nights a week at £17 10s per night.

'A four-piece band would set you a cut above your competitors,' Ray pointed out, trusting in the lack of competition.

'We feel confident that our musical and communicative abilities would fill the club on a fairly regular basis,' I put in.

The committee debated this proposition behind locked doors for a week. The working men's club quorum was four members, but a massive decision like this one demanded more than four brains, so a special meeting was held to agonize over the matter. Would we be worth the risk? Would we pull in a large audience and still leave enough money for the committee to go to the Costa Brava at the end of it all or would they be content with their usual day trip to Blackpool?

After a week's waiting, we saw white smoke come out of the committee room ... *Habemus bandus, Rayus Martinus.* We got the job and played some Latin music which the members thoroughly enjoyed. After three months with us the British Legionnaires could do the cha-cha and the tango better than most, thanks to the strict tempos and disciplines of the Ray Martin Sound which filled the club.

Actually, it was more of a hangar than a club. The ceiling was so high you couldn't see it and the Red Arrows did the second half. The room was cavernous and only served to heighten the musical imperfections of our band, although Ray Martin and the boys were good musicians. As compère I used to make the announcements, tell a few gags and in the twelve-month period we were there I managed to hone some degree of comedic skills. A residency in a club stretched the imagination of the performer in no small way. Different material had to found every week and I suppose my time there served me well in later life when I had to face far more critical audiences.

Phyllis came to the British Legion every night and sat with the bass player's wife, Chris. A few weeks into the summer season of 1969 we had to save them four chairs because they needed two each to sit on comfortably; both were in a condition that heightened our sense of responsibility – very pregnant. As Phyllis was expecting a baby and we decided she should stop supply teaching, so my evening bookings became a more important part of our income.

I never fitted in the pacing-up-and-down-hospital-corridors routine but on the evening of 1 December I did pace the stage at the Ocean Caravan Park. Pinky and Perky would have been proud of my speedy rendition of *Cherry Pink* that night. When the gig was over I hurried to the telephone to contact the maternity ward for a progress report.

Elated by what I heard I put down the phone, reached for my pint, and gazed into the clouds of cigarette smoke which hung over the audience. The smoke turned white and sig-nalled *Habemus Papa!* (We have a Dad!) which I announced on the microphone. Not being very good at Latin, the audi-ence thought the pies had come and started milling round to find them. I phoned the hospital back two minutes later to make sure it was true and it hadn't been an imagined appar-ition. An amused matron confirmed the good news: 'You have a lovely little girl and Phyllis is fine.'

I zipped off to the hospital and checked that there were two of everything, then went back home and checked my diary to make sure I was booked solid until Christmas. There was now a pressing need for regular evening work, an extra mouth to feed and all that jazz. Whoopee!

I managed to visit the hospital every night after my stint with the band, but that wasn't a lot of use to Phyllis as I usually arrived when she was asleep. Sometimes I managed breakfast with the nurses.

Phyllis has never made a fuss or a drama about anything; she has the knack of somehow enjoying life without drama and is at the heart of everything that is beautiful about my life. Even choosing our baby's name was a doddle. We had made the decision about children's names on the day we got married, based on three main criteria: firstly that the child should be named after no one in particular so they had a name to make their own; secondly that it shouldn't be a name that would be a burden to them in the form of spelling out, justifying or translating; thirdly that it shouldn't lend itself to a ridiculous nickname. To fit the bill exactly, Susan and Peter were the names that we had chosen for our children as long ago as our honeymoon. I suppose the world would be a repetitive place if we were surrounded by Toms and Bills and Sues and Petes, but each to their own.

By New Man standards I wasn't a model first-time father. When we took Sue out for her first Christmas, I managed to drop her in the White Lion at Holton, but only a few inches. Phyllis accused me of being drunk in charge of a carrycot and it never happened again.

I kept my New Year's resolution to learn how to change a nappy and was given a lesson by Phyllis in the living room. I was petrified, I handled our baby like a precious Ming vase and by the time I'd completed the operation, the nappy needed changing again. However, I'd learned how to do it, as promised, just in case I ever needed to change a nappy in an emergency. An emergency never arose.

My role as a father was as a provider; I was far better at

telling gags and bringing money home than I was at fumbling about with nappies at home when Phyllis did it so capably. Our division of labour was never a problem. It was the way we had always planned it.

Phyllis did notice that Sue cried if a man looked at her in her pram and we decided this was because, for the first three months of her life, she really didn't see much of me. I only got to look at her when she was asleep. I was a good father, and even though my daughter didn't know I was her dad until she could talk, she knew that I brought home the bootees.

Our daughter Sue was about one month old when it became clear to me that she probably wouldn't be growing up with the burden of a headmaster as a father, because St Paul released me from his primary school in Caton with a timely admonition from the school governors:

'Look Jim, if you're going to be a headmaster you've got to stop the evening work. We can't have you working at Salford British Legion telling the story about naughty ladies on a Sunday night and taking assembly Monday morning singing *Oh Worship The King*. The two are not compatible.'

I bought that, it was fair. I was working in two worlds that were poles apart, and I got the message that if I didn't relinquish my ties with showbusines I was not going to climb any further up the career ladder in education. So I jumped off the headmaster train and dived into clubland. It would have been far more frightening if there hadn't been so much work around, but I had been offered a job as manager of the Morecambe Bowl and I took it.

The owners of Morecambe Bowl, the McAnulty brothers, Joe and Dennis, had heard about the success of the Ray Martin Sound with yours truly compèring. By now I was working with them for the lovely George Hitchen at the Ocean Edge Caravan Park, where we enjoyed tremendous success. We had built up a lively cabaret scene over a relatively short period of time, and the McAnulty brothers approached me to do the same at Morecambe Bowl, a big cabaret venue.

I thought management might be another career opportunity for me, but the venture lasted only a few months because my heart wasn't in it. I became more firmly convinced that my place was behind the microphone. I would rather do an act myself than book one. And during my four months of management duties, I really missed the laughter. It was more than a full-time job, it was double time. I was working round the clock and Sue and Phyllis saw even less of me.

I'd kept in touch with the world of education and quickly got back into teaching through supply work, replacing the teachers who had caught flu or something worse in the club the night before. I did a spell of maths teaching at one Skerton school in Lancaster (known as the Skerton Shirtoff School) and enjoyed the place so much that when a permanent job fell vacant I applied, only to learn that making something of a name for myself as a club comic was having a negative effect on my reputation as a teacher.

Miss Bailey, the headmistress, quietly informed me that one of the school governors had primly but firmly opposed my application with the words, 'I believe Mr Whittaker goes out at night telling smutty jokes.'

That wasn't quite true. I told stories that were smutty in *her* view but in fact I pride myself on never having told a dirty joke. I don't remember much at all about the school governor who was so opposed to telling jokes, but she must have been considered in some way equipped to make decisions of academic consequence. Ah yes, I think she ran a fish and chip shop.

It was true, however, that I worked at night and I'd never tried to hide it, although by now I was getting used to the fact that school governors would not judge me by my teaching alone. And I was aware that my classroom technique involved some valuable skills not always evident in the contributions of school governors. If the children knew that I worked as a different kind of performer in the evenings, I didn't feel that it detracted from my performance as a teacher.

A stand-up comic commands a presence. He has to. And you can't develop a presence in front of a class of children or an audience of adults by going on and being ethereal. In a working men's club, firstly they don't know what ethereal means and secondly they have no time to find out in between ordering the pints and getting the biro out of the knicker elastic for the next game of bingo. You've got to hit 'em hard and grab 'em quick, and when you've got their attention you aim to make them shut their mail order catalogues and stop selling tea-sets while you are standing up there to establish yourself. That was my training ground and it was an abrasive experience that made the next club audience a more enjoyable challenge than a board of school governors.

When you've done Manchester Labour Club, hell fire, you can handle Salford Conservatives, but you keep in store the speed and reflex actions that you've learned.

There are corresponding skills in a teacher's performance. Ben Johnson could stand on stage as head of 700 boys at Accrington Boys Grammar and he had a presence – basically the pupils were frightened to ruddy death of him – but he still had a presence. That's not the sort of presence you want as a comic, but it is the sort of presence you get by working and working.

I had broken the serious shackles of my childhood by walking on stages and making audiences laugh, and knew that I wanted to go on entertaining people. Some are born to perform, some are made, and I just drifted into it, I wasn't pushed by circumstances. Unfortunately I never got the chance to ask the Sherton school governor what she did at night because I had landed myself a booking for a whole week at the Dolphin Bar at Cleveleys.

14

The Comedians

It was a Wednesday night at the Dolphin in 1971 when I heard coming from the audience a very strange, long-forgotten sound which I thankfully recognized as laughter. To this day I don't know why I got laughs on the Wednesday, because I'd used the same material eight times that week and not even heard a cheerful cough. That very morning, facing the prospect of another silent night, I'd resigned myself to finding an audience more responsive to my talents by becoming a welder or a vicar. Then suddenly I got laughs.

The big bonus of working at the Dolphin had been the compère, the late Brian Rossi, who exuded charm and insanity from every pore. Brian was king at the Dolphin and the comic came second. He spoke incredibly quickly in a heavy-duty Irish brogue, understood only by the inebriated. People would come to see him again and again, because he was so outrageous and because it took a minimum of four visits to decipher him. Then they could bring their friends to see him and be able to translate all his jokes.

Brian always said he discovered me because he booked me that week and had a hard time persuading the owners of the Dolphin to take me again, but in fact it was another, more lucid Irishman who thrust me into the public eye: Frank Carson.

After that singularly successful Wednesday performance, I

walked to the back of the room to wait for my next spot. You didn't get a dressing room at the Dolphin, but if you wanted a door to close behind you there was always the broom cupboard. So I stood at the bar and there I beheld Frank Carson, who lived in Blackpool at the time and had called in for a drink. He was a big star. If I'd known he was in the audience I would probably have plunged back into the downward spiral of silent audience nights; if he'd known I was on he would undoubtedly have chosen to drink at the Clifton.

'I enjoyed that, Jim,' he said. 'Granada television are doing a programme about comedians all doing gags. Do you want to be in it?'

What a question to ask a comedian who had just had his first successful night in weeks. The nearest I had ever been to a television contract was signing a three-year agreement with Radio Rentals for a fourteen-inch black and white set. And here was a whiff of hope from someone who turned out to be a man of his word.

'Brilliant,' I said. 'You can get in touch with me on ...'

'I'll find you when they want you,' Frank cut in.

Anybody who comes up to you and says they've been talking to Frank Carson has got to be telling huge porkies, because you don't talk to Frank, you just listen. He's very proud of his position as Mayor of Balbriggan and it is a well-known fact that there are more three-legged donkeys in Balbriggan than anywhere else on the planet. The missing hind legs have been stolen by Frank Carson. Luckily for me, that night at the Dolphin was one of the rare times in his life when Frank hadn't kissed the blarney stone. (In fact, Frank, I think you've since swallowed it!)

Frank Carson was showing me a gateway to paradise. A hint of television in 1971 was like manna from heaven; television could make you a star, unlike today when there are so many channels that one appearance doesn't mean a light. Yet without the genuine belief that it's going to happen for them, nobody would be in the business. There are hundreds of comics and singers up and down the nation who are convinced that they are going to be discovered and that's the only reason they get up in working men's clubs on Friday nights to 300 legless patrons and sing *Ten Guitars*. The sounds they are hoping to hear are those of the telephone ringing and an agent saying, 'Palladium. Next Friday.'

Now I felt I was almost touching a dream. I waited impatiently for the call; every time the phone rang I leaped through the air, but it was either the Four Star agency in Liverpool offering me the usual ten pounds a night or an offer of supply teaching.

There had still been no word from Granada when the first series of 'The Comedians' came out in June 1971, and I might have given up hope if the programme hadn't been such a phenomenal success. I sat spellbound – it was fresh, hilarious and such a simple idea. By the third programme it had stormed the country and was bigger than 'Coronation Street'. On Fridays the pubs weren't bothering to open until 'The Comedians' had finished.

The series ended and I'd still heard nothing, except a kind offer from a Miss Ascott, headmistress of a local school which dealt with children with learning difficulties. She took a chance with me after I'd done some supply teaching for her and gave me a full-time job in Morecambe at Sunnyfield School. My usual drill applied to the special children in Class 4: we're going to win, right? We developed the painting and illustrated a lot of work, we put on shows for other classes. There was a competent team of teachers in that school. I taught the class under the supervision of Brian Wellock, a very supportive deputy head with whom I'd qualified at Chester College in 1959. I enjoyed the smaller classes and the different challenges involved with giving more time to children with learning difficulties.

Then one frosty February evening in 1972 the call came from the Four Star agency. Would I go down to Manchester and record 'The Comedians'? I spent the weekend getting some jokes together, staying awake, worrying, drinking coffee and being a complete drag with Phyllis, until we drove over and met Johnnie Hamp, the director and one of nature's gentlemen.

I didn't really know what was wanted so I just did my usual stuff, rambling on telling long stories and going back to the original gag. The first one I did was about the Vikings: two men with horns on their head, beards, bacon round their necks and Danish stamped on their chests going round the country asking people in different towns if they've been raped and pillaged because they can't find their mates. It went on for about nine minutes and pulled the place to pieces.

'It's funny,' said Johnnie Hamp, 'but I can't use that. Go away and get some short gags.'

I wasn't too disillusioned by my unusable recording for 'The Comedians', because everybody had been laughing and Phyllis said that Frank Carson had been peeping round to see how I was doing. But I didn't know many short gags. I didn't know many gags at all; in my brief career as a comic I'd grown used to making all the jokes I knew fill a twenty-minute slot by spinning them out and adding padding lines such as, 'Dip your bread in and tell 'em nothing,' 'Let 'em buy a programme,' 'Smack my leg and call me Richard,' and, still popular in the days of wayward bishops, 'Are you staying for the prayer meeting later?'

I had to learn the technique of doing short gags and I went back to the recordings of the shows again and again until eventually I came up with one about Cecil B. de Mille shooting a horribly expensive movie with a burning building in the middle of a forest and being left with embers and no film. The first time I did the joke it lasted thirteen minutes twenty seconds, which was more than half the programme, in which time they would have told thirty or forty jokes. So I did it again and got it down to eight minutes, then seven, and eventually I raced like mad and they transmitted it at four minutes.

For weeks I'd been phoning Granada anonymously every Wednesday to ask for a list of the comics appearing on

'The Comedians' on the following Friday. I usually spoke to Johnnie Hamp's assistant, Lucinda, aka the Brilliant Loo. When she eventually read out my name I set down the phone and ran round the house looking in mirrors.

I was coming off stage in Preston when I saw myself on 'The Comedians' for the first time, on the television set in the bar. Johnnie Hamp had obviously seen some promise about me before he asked me back, but I didn't think I'd done all that well. Nevertheless, the next morning I got up early and went out to walk tall around Morecambe in the hope of being asked for my autograph. I remembered hearing Alec Guinness explaining on radio how he managed to walk about in the West End without being recognized. He said that the trick was to look down and avoid direct eye contact at all costs. I strode up and down the promenade ninety-five times eyeballing the world and looking for the smallest reaction. I stared at lamp-posts, praying for movement. I peered at elderly holiday makers as if the meaning of life were shining from their eyes. I got a few more smiles than I deserved, but no spark of recognition. I was just a wild-looking stranger peering at them through thick glasses.

'That man keeps looking at you, Arthur. Does he go in the Queen's Head?'

'Walk on, Edna, walk on. I think he's a bit simple ...'

When I have a little yearning for anonymity now, I remember those heady days and that thirst for fame. I was about as recognizable as a lump of earth from Mars.

Johnnie Hamp must have been satisfied with something I'd done because he said I could go back whenever I liked. And I liked a lot. Johnnie is one of the few people in my book of heroes. He is undoubtedly one of the greatest programme makers in the history of television and also a good accountant. Having scoured the country and looked at five hundred or so comedians, he would get ten guys, pay us £75 each for twelve minutes and he had a two-hour show for £750. In the days when you needed a crane and three strong men to move a camera, he used only three for the whole programme. We would walk on, stand on a little podium, tell the gags, then roll quickly on with the laughter to the next comic

To warm up the audience and introduce the show Johnnie got Shep's Banjo Band to play exotic music, mostly *When You're Smiling*. The band were eventually able to leave their non-musical day jobs thanks to the offers of work they received after 'The Comedians'.

I had come into the programme on the second wave. The first division included people such as Bernard Manning, Colin Crompton, George Roper, Mike Burton – a very funny man, probably the master of the one-liner. Mike and I looked very much alike at the time and people would mistake us for brothers, which was useful in bars. I used to go and watch Mike work and learned a lot from him and, of course, Bernard, but you don't watch Bernard, you just stand well back. Frank Carson was there every week, simply being his outrageous self. They all had great infectious laughs, particularly Bryn Phillips, a Welshman with lovely teeth. Then there was Stevie Faye, Ken Goodwin and Charlie Williams, the only black Yorkshireman who's never been down a pit. He could tell gags about coloured people that the rest of us couldn't without having the 'Save the Ferret in Mansfield' brigade knocking on the door and complaining about racism. He used to say, 'If tha don't laugh at this joke, I'll come and live next door to thee.'

We also had a lot of fun with the cards, known as idiot boards, where we wrote our list of jokes for the night.

'What am I doing today, Phyllis?' I'd ask my wife, as I do most days, on the drive to Manchester. We'd choose some jokes, write them on the card as soon as we got to the studio and then hide it in the dressing room, because if anyone saw your card and went on before you they were likely to try out one of your jokes. Bernard Manning might pop his nose round the dressing-room door and say, 'Oh yes, that's funny, the one about the doctor and the swollen foot. I'll have that.'

There was once a technical breakdown when Bernard was finishing his spot and George Roper was due on next. Johnnie called out, 'Can you just give us a couple more minutes, Bernard, until we get this camera fixed?'

'Right, here we go,' said Bernard, grinning broadly as his eyes landed on George Roper's card. He talked to the audience, did all George's jokes, then, when the camera was ready to roll, he said, 'Right, now here's a very funny man, George Roper.' And George had to go on with no material and swim.

In the Mafioso of 'The Comedians' Bernard was Legs Diamond and Johnnie Hamp was Al Capone. At that stage I was in training to be a mere getaway car driver.

The secret was to get on early so you had your choice of gags. Bernard always had to go on first so he could get back to his own club in Manchester (The Embassy Club, so renowned for its lavish style that everyone knows you have to wipe your feet on the way out). And the rest of us used to make up appointments: 'I've got a booking in Southampton tonight, Johnnie. Can I go on soon?'

Johnnie would put us where he wanted to. He had the last word and we knew he would create the best possible programme. Everybody looked forward to it, there was no competition and all the comics were made very welcome, which was a reflection of Johnnie's skill. He used to say, 'Come on, lads, just give us some one minutes, give us some thirty seconds.' We knew at the end of the day Al Capone would get it right.

'Get Jim out of Studio Three,' he'd say if I wasn't there when he wanted me. Studio Three was the fond pseudonym we gave to the Film Exchange bar in Deansgate, Manchester, a convenient 800 yards from the studios. There was no drink allowed on the Granada premises because of the ruling from Sidney Bernstein, head of Granada Television. So I used to pack three or four pints down before a show and even try and sneak bottles past the security men. I was under the mistaken impression that alcohol would help me to relax before appearing in front of eighteen million people. The more experienced comics knew better and would wait until we'd finished work before heading for Studio Three to loosen their tongues with abandon. And a fine time was had by all.

One of our favourite running jokes concerned fellow comedian Eddie Flanagan's wife. Sadly, dear Eddie Flanagan is dead now, but I'm sure he wouldn't mind my telling this story as a memento of all the good times we shared in the Film Exchange.

One night when Eddie was working in a club in Manchester he offered to give two strippers a lift home to save them waiting for the night bus. His wife, a sweet woman whose naïvety was often a bit of an embarrassment to Eddie, was in the car. She thought the strippers were charming girls and they were having a good old chat on the drive home when it turned out that one of the strippers bred poodles.

'Oh, we've got a poodle,' said Mrs Flanagan. 'We got it from Lita Roza, you know that lovely woman who sings with the Ted Heath Orchestra.'

'Is that the one who's a bit bent?' said the stripper.

'Well, she probably got it off her dad,' said Eddie's wife. 'He had a bit of a stoop.'

It was just one long hoot for us, and I think that's one reason why the series ran as long as it did, because it was obvious that everyone was having a great time. And another thing it did was to gobble gags and make comedians work harder at their acts. You couldn't just go out and do gags that you were doing in the pub because they had been on the box. You had to develop a technique to offset the fact that the gag had already been told, by telling it a different way or putting in catchphrases.

Johnnie Hamp didn't look for stars, he made them. It was said that I was one of his favourites and I take that as a great compliment because Johnnie is a man who really knows his comedy. One of the lovely things about working with him was that he made us all feel like his favourite. In the three years of 'The Comedians' he always appeared to enjoy having us all around him, and when it was his turn on 'This Is Your

Life' in 1993 it showed: all 'his' comics came on and he was so proud of us all, even me in the second division. My Bentley and my swimming pool are all down to Johnnie Hamp, and, I suppose, a few hundred thousand miles of driving from club to club each year in an attempt to take advantage of the opportunity he gave me.

15

A Murmur in Court

I had been teaching at Sunnyfield for about six months and was getting along fine, when one day a pupil in my class called Anthea was extremely rude to me, so rude in fact that I felt it warranted a smack on the leg. She went home and told her mum and students at a local university heard of the incident and made the mother aware of the possibility of taking legal action against me. I was at that time appearing on Granada Television's 'The Comedians', so I suppose my almost parochial fame made me fair game as a nice little publicity stunt for the students.

Weeks later Miss Ascott called me into her office to tell me that the police would be arriving in half an hour to charge me with assault.

Anthea's mum was a lovely lady, a working mother, single parent I believe, coping with a child with learning difficulties. She led a difficult life and I really think she had many other axes to grind, but she had been influenced by this student faction at the local university. It appeared to be a student-inspired action because when I stood in court facing Anthea's mother and a solicitor for the prosecution who had been specially shipped in from Manchester, there was a handful of students behind me whose demeanour spoke of con-frontation.

All the work I had done with the kids seemed to count for

nothing in that room. Nobody there really knew or cared about what I'd done with Class 4 at Sunnyfield. I had had to find my own solicitor and the obvious choice was the man who had handled our house purchasing since our arrival in the area. He seemed quite adequate to this naïve defendant. I looked round the court for some professional presence, but no. In 1972 when you smacked a child no one wanted to be present. You just hadn't to be there! The only person in court with any connection with education at all, apart from me, was a man called George Tomlinson, a very nice NUT man who was headmaster of a nearby primary school.

'How do you plead, Mr Whittaker?'

'Not guilty.'

'Did you smack the pupil.'

'Yes I did.'

'Did you intend to hurt her?'

'Yes I did. There would have been no point in my smacking her if I wasn't going to hurt her.'

'Why did you use this form of punishment?'

'I'd rather not say what she said to me, but she was very rude to me and she knows she was very rude to me.'

'Did Mr Whittaker hurt you, Anthea?'

'No, not really,' she said, because the girl didn't know what it was about.

'Mr Whittaker, would you administer this form of punishment again?'

'Yes, I definitely would. If you think I'm going to say no to get me out of this, you're wrong. I can't do that. If Anthea said that to me again, I would do exactly the same thing and she knows that.'

'Do you realize that this is assault?'

'If you like. Call it what you want. I smacked her on the back of her leg, on the calf to be precise, and if she spoke to me like that again I'd smack her leg again with exactly the same intent. If you choose to call that assault, I'm sorry. But it might interest you to know that she never actually said it to me again, so I think she may well have learned something from that smack. We're talking about a learning process here. She was certainly in no way physically or mentally damaged.

The prosecuting counsel said, 'Anthea. Did Mr Whittaker hurt you?'

Anthea looked towards me for the answer, and I nodded to encourage her to speak. I looked at her standing in the dock and thought: how cruel to stand a child on a stage like that and ask her questions about something that happened months ago. It was ludicrous. I found myself nodding to encourage her to come out with an answer.

Her answer came, 'No, not really. I don't think so.'

There was a murmur in the court and the prosecuting council turned to my solicitor, they muttered a bit and I awaited the magistrates' decision. (I found out afterwards that the prosecuting solicitor had said that there was no point in carrying on, he no longer believed there was a case to answer.)

The magistrates dismissed the case.

I walked out of the court room and straight to the Education Offices in Lancaster and sought audience with the chief education officer.

'I'm a bit disappointed about this. There was nobody in that court room this morning from my school, your office or from anybody in the education establishment to support me. What would have happened if I'd been found guilty?'

'Oh,' he said. 'You'd have been on your own.'

'I can see that my track record doesn't come into this. My twelve years' teaching, the films, the modern version of *The Crucifixion* I did at Caton Primary, the exhibition work, students who have been given As for their teaching practices ... that all counts for nothing in this situation.

'Pay me until today and I won't be at work tomorrow. Put in a sub, get somebody off the bench, because I'm out of the game.'

I came out of the teaching profession deeply disillusioned. It was the end of an era, and from then on it's been showbiz all the way.

16

Clacton Pier Pressure

I never regretted leaving teaching for the world of humour and laughter. I wouldn't like to work in a school now, I'd be no good at all because I wouldn't tolerate the pupils' behaviour or the way schools are run. 'The Comedians' had given me a high enough profile to keep the bookings coming in, but clubland was still recovering from the effects of the three-day week of the previous winter, so it wasn't the easiest time for a stand-up comic to spread his wings.

Clacton pier featured heavily in my diary for 1973, as I was booked for 'The Comedians' Summer Show there, in my first year as a full-time performer with no supply teaching to balance my life and my income.

We did so much business on Clacton pier that summer, it was a cure for agoraphobia. Looking out from the stage to the back of the auditorium night after night I used to be able to say 'I've slept with more people than we've got in the audience tonight, and I'm not even good at it.' I was pleased to be there but I could have had as much fun spending summer evenings gazing at an empty fridge. Russ Abbot was there in his first season as a solo comedian. Then there was Sammy Thomas, the short-tongued black comedian who would walk on stage and say, 'I've just come back from the touth of Franth, can you not tell from the tan?' We all got accustomed to working to a large empty space and soon a whole row of full seats was something to be eagerly reported backstage as a cause for major excitement.

One Wednesday evening in August we were particularly high-spirited before the curtain went up because we had been told that the audience was well into three figures – about 300 seats had been filled, which meant that the theatre was a quarter full and made it the best Wednesday night we'd had so far.

Comedian Pat Mooney was performing when a man in green overalls dashed in front of him and yelled, 'Don't panic, ladies and gentlemen. Don't panic. The pier is on fire! The Cyclone's gone up!'

The whole audience replied in one voice – 'Aaaaaagh!' and scrambled out of their seats. Grabbing the microphone from Pat's hands, the demented green-overalled man screamed, 'There's no need to rush. Please don't rush. Don't fight to get out. PLEASE stay CALM ladies and gentlemen.' But it was too late, because 1,200 limbs were already flying in every direction. The theatre is situated halfway along Clacton pier and nobody was stopping to ask which end was on fire. The sheer desperation in the voice of the inexperienced fire officer was enough to give anyone who wasn't a woman or a child the sudden knowledge that they ought to be.

Comic Jimmy Marshall, who had just bought a new car, was first out of the stage door with the words, 'Where's my effing Bentley?' and he moved along the pier very purposefully in order to rescue his vehicle. Next day he was reported in the press as having dashed from the theatre to save lives.

We were sick because we had missed the opportunity to work to a proper audience and there was absolutely no chance of getting them back into the theatre. If only we could have led them out in orderly fashion and then marched them back in when the all-clear was given, perhaps even picked up a few more on the way. As it was, we had little choice but to sit in a nearby hotel bar to drown our sorrows and watch our potentially record-breaking audience queue up to get a refund on their tickets, too traumatized to think of booking for another night. I think it was the same summer as that terrible fire tragedy at Summerland on the Isle of Wight, where people were killed when a plastic building caught fire, so there was no persuading anyone back into the theatre.

There's another warm memory of that summer in Clacton, too. One evening a member of the audience with a vaguely familiar face came to see me after the show.

'Hello, I enjoyed the show. How are things with you, Jim?' he asked, obviously expecting me to remember him from somewhere.

'Er, fine thanks. What about you ...?' I said, trying to place this enthusiastic stranger. Then the penny dropped and I didn't like where it landed. This was none other than a long-established member of my Obliterati, last seen six years ago when interviewing for the same job as me. It was the man who had helped me stay out of lecturing in 1967.

'Oh, could be better really,' winged the lecturer. 'I've just been made redundant from the college.'

'Really, what a shame,' I said, 'I really am upset about that. I suppose that means you're out of work. I'm sorry but I've got to dash off because I'm taking Phyllis out to dinner and I've got to pick up the Merc ...'

My chance meeting with an Obliterati made me feel a very lucky man, not least because Phyllis and I had something very special to celebrate that night. We were expecting another child.

Our son Peter was born the following spring. Sue was now four and old enough to share the excitement in that she knew her mother would be coming out of hospital with a baby brother or sister for her.

Phyllis's Mum was staying with us and was standing with me in the office at home when the phone rang. She was standing by my left shoulder, hoping to hear the happy news.

'This is the Royal Lancaster Infirmary, Mr Whittaker. You've got a little boy and your wife is fine, but can you come down to the hospital?'

That word 'but' raised the biggest question mark of my life.

'Yes, of course I'm coming down to the hospital. Are Phyllis and the baby okay? Is something wrong?'

'Just come down as soon as you can, Mr Whittaker.'

I turned to Mrs Owen to say, 'It's a boy! But ... just a minute ...' I'll never forget the anxiety on her face.

I went back to the phone. 'Please don't be like this, sister. If something is wrong, please tell me now, then I'm coming straight over to see you.'

'Well, the baby has a harelip. Apart from that everything's in perfect working order,' said the sister.

'Oh. Well, we can put that right, can't we?'

'Yes, we can put that right in a few weeks.'

'No problem then. Thank you for telling me. I'm on my way.' I put down the receiver, knowing that this would be difficult news for Mrs Owen to take.

Before I could explain to her she said, 'The baby's got a harelip, hasn't he?'

She had guessed because her family had a history of harelips. Her brother, one of her sons (who had died during a corrective operation years before) and her youngest daughter all had harelips, yet the family had been told it was not hereditary!

I really didn't want Phyllis and her mother to feel responsible. I said to Mrs Owen in the car on the way to the hospital, 'Please don't worry. The doctors will be much more experienced with this kind of surgery than they were when you lost your son. And there isn't the social stigma that you might have had to deal with years ago.

'You know, my being adopted means that there could be sixty harelips in my family and I wouldn't know; there could be a whole generation of them and I might be the only one who has escaped. And there are some people who think I should not have a hole where my mouth is at all!'

Because of that awful moment on the phone I had prepared myself for the worst, by the time I got to see my new son, he looked absolutely wonderful to me. Everything was in the right place and he was perfect apart from a big hole in his face. We can laugh about it now because he's always been so handsome, on a good day.

'What's all the trauma about?' I asked the nurse. 'He's got everything a body needs, all in working order. Who can we talk to about fixing the harelip?'

The surgeon came to speak to us that evening to explain exactly what could be done and we booked Pete in for the operation in three weeks' time. Meanwhile we took our son home and Phyllis's Mum asked, 'Can we have the christening before the operation?' Her concern was so touching that we speedily organized the christening before Pete had his major repair work done. I really wish that Pete could remember his christening party, because a fine time was had by all. I had asked Johnnie Hamp to be Pete's godfather and only learned after he'd left the party early that he had travelled from Geneva and back in twenty-four hours to keep his promise. It was unlike Johnnie to disappear before dawn and I thought it strange that he left quite early, but it was just like him not to tell me he was working in Geneva.

Phyllis walked the pram around the village, dealing with the little problem with her usual style and tact. It brought to mind my mother's stories of how she'd had to answer questions about suddenly revealing me in a pram in Clayton-le-Moors. Except with Phyllis it was a question of volunteering information before anyone looked in the pram, so there would be no embarrassed coughing outside the post office.

Sue was delighted with her little brother and had no problem with the idea that every now and then he had to be taken to the hospital to be mended a bit.

The major work for Pete was done at Sharoe Green Hospital when he was about three months old. The surgeon, Mr Maurice, did a brilliant job on Pete's lip. Magnificent. Changed my son's life. I am eternally grateful to the staff there and wanted to offer a little gift to the ward as a token of our appreciation.

'Excuse me, sister,' I said to the ward boss. 'Is there anything you want for the ward, something that the children would like?'

'Well, I didn't say this, Mr Whittaker,' she said with a grin. (I was a little twinkly star then and most people at the hospital knew they could have a joke with me.) 'We'd love an aquarium in the ward so the children can watch the fish, but the matron said we can't have one because we haven't the time to maintain it properly.'

'Well, I'd say that one of those self-cleaning tanks would fit the bill,' I ventured, and the sister nodded excitedly. 'I've seen one with a pump in the shape of a diver who spends all day cleaning the tank. Now, we haven't had this conversation.' The sister shook her head enthusiastically. 'I'm sure matron will love it when it arrives.'

Funny coincidence, but I think somewhere in that hospital today there's an aquarium with a brass plate hidden underneath that reads, 'Thanks from Pete.' Because I happen to know that in 1974 the tank was delivered in a van and quickly installed along with pump, heater and fish by men in white overalls. One of the delivery men bore an uncanny resemblance to a friend of mine called Mort Allan, famous businessman, compère, singer, heckler and wrestler of our parish, who trimmed his moustache especially for the role and assured me that access and installation were easily achieved by repeating the words, 'Manchester Regional Hospital Board Technical Services, delivery of tank for Ward Four. We've got to get a move on because we've got another one to take to Blackpool before teatime.'

Mort can be very convincing – he has even convinced people that he used to eat raw rabbits – so even the matron asked no further questions.

When the matron of Sharoe Green Hospital came to see me in cabaret some years later she asked, 'How's your son Peter? His tank is still going strong.'

I thought Pete was coming on strong as well, but with the hindsight that I suppose carries painful parts for most parents, I can see that his early years were spent in the shadow of his elder sister. One day in 1977 stands out particularly, when Stuart Hall came to stay for the weekend. Stuart, a dear friend of mine who directed 'This Is Your Life', is full of fun and was one of the children's favourite guests because he always made a lot of time for them.

Sue and Pete ran to meet him at the station and were delighted when he got off the train wearing a white German helmet, carrying a stiffened lead with an empty collar and talking to an invisible dog.

When we all got home Sue took Stuart up to her room to look at the latest rosettes she'd won on her pony. She wasn't boasting, but Stuart always encouraged her to tell him about what she'd been up to. 'This one I got for coming second, this one I fell off and got back on, here's a picture of me doing gymnastics, oh and I've got my first ballet exam, and there's a picture of Twinkle and me, and this is the best cup, the one that I won last week . . .'

Then into the room toddled Pete, who looked up at Sue and Stuart and said, 'I've got a Jubilee mug.'

Every child in the village had a Jubilee mug. And this scene crystallizes for me the way I think my son grew up in my daughter's shadow. Although Pete himself says he never felt as if he were in anyone's shadow, when problems come round in the teenage years you look back for reasons and this is where I know I was guilty. It's no good getting the eldest child on the right road and then thinking the next one will happily follow, because each child needs to be helped along their own road. I don't regret working at weekends, because that was the life we'd chosen and Phyllis was happy to go from being a groom with Sue to a mechanic with Pete when he got into motocross, with me turning up to watch whenever I could. But I now feel I should have spent more time talking to Pete, sticking to his individual case. As it was I made the classic mistake in the fatherhood routine of stepping in hard when things started to go wrong.

The biggest warning sign came for me one night at the

Scarthwaite Hotel where I met my friends Bob and Daphne. They asked after my family and I mentioned that Pete was doing fine.

'Who's Pete?' asked Bob.

'Pete, you know Pete, my son,' I said, thinking I'd missed a joke.

'Jim, you've never told us about him,' Daphne explained. 'We know all about Sue and her horseriding and everything, but you've really never mentioned that you had two children.'

This couple had known me for six years, they knew I had a daughter and knew every detail about her, but I'd never told them a thing about Pete. I hated myself.

I'm not writing anything that I haven't told my children, and luckily for me they assure me they bear me no grudges. They are now sufficiently grown up to look back and laugh at life with me as a dad. But later in Pete's life I was to share a great deal of grief with a lot of other parents whose children change the course of their lives by using drugs, so I know that there is a useful place for looking back and putting one's mistakes as a parent in context.

17

Southern Comfort

'The Comedians' stopped temporarily in 1974 and the following year Johnnie quickly brought out a series called 'The Wheeltappers and Shunters Social Club'. It used the working men's club scenario as a vehicle for different acts, so he invited all his comedians back. I once played my trumpet on 'Wheeltappers' and had to follow Ronnie Dukes and Rikki Lee, who were probably the best cabaret act on the circuit. Wherever they went they stopped the show and that night they were phenomenal. As I stood waiting to go on my trumpet was trembling.

I said to Johnnie, 'I can't do this. How will I do better than that?'

'Trust me,' said Johnnie. 'Never follow a bad act.'

He was right, of course. If you follow a bad act you have to lift the audience, but if you are halfway decent and you follow a good act you can get in on the top and use that atmosphere that they've created and perform.

I won't say I did just as well as Ronnie Dukes and Rikki Lee, but I certainly did okay. I played – guess what? – *Cherry Pink*, with the band out of tune behind me, which was quite comforting, as it sounded similar to the time I'd played the same song at the Padiham fleshpot back in the 50s.

'When did you start to play the trumpet, Jim?' asked Bernard Manning when I'd finished.

'I only started last Saturday,' I told him.

'I know that, what ferking time?'

Bernard used to compère 'Wheeltappers' and insult every-body, swearing all the time in the knowledge that Johnnie would be able to cut it out. One of his most memorable introductions went something like this: 'I reckon this man was responsible for starting the Second World War. He was over in Germany in 1939 and Hitler heard him playing the piano. Orders were given to find out the pianist's nationality and when Hitler discovered where he was from he said, "Right, we'll bomb the bastards." Here he is, Joe Mr Piano Henderson.'

Bernard had lines such as, 'Now this next act ... I've seen better turns in Manchester eye hospital,' and the whole studio would be laughing before the act started.

Batley Variety Club, Wakefield Theatre Club and the Fiesta in Sheffield were my weekly round, but I wanted more club work so I started looking further afield.

I was one of the few northern comics who had no trouble making the north–south transition and I found myself driving down to London more and more often. I love London audiences and soon realized that if I just slowed down my speech a little there was no need to temper the accent. Southerners generally tend to be slightly more civilized in that they give you longer to prove yourself. Oh, they'll let you know if they don't like you, but it's unlikely to be during the first five minutes of your act.

The further north you go, the harder the audiences get. In the north-east if you haven't got 'em in the first two minutes it's time to start the car. (Now there's a generalization that tempts providence; it could even result in my working for long stretches in Iceland.)

Luckily I had the help of an agency called North Come South, run by Jack Sharpe who lived in Basildon. Jack loved comics and he would rally me, Douggie Brown and Charlie Williams to come down to London for a week of one-nighters.

One-spot bookings would have left us out of pocket on the journey beyond Watford, whereas the boys in London only had to travel fifteen miles across London to earn £50. The first job I ever did for Jack Sharpe was the Marconi Social Club at Chelmsford, a beautiful club, and I did well enough to be invited back. Dustin Gee and I spent many a week in illustrious £30-a-week digs in Wanstead. We tried to book weekday evenings so we could leave at five in the morning on Saturday, for the weekend at home. As my daughter Sue had grown into a terribly busy eight-year-old, my Saturday timetable involved trying to get home in time to watch her riding in the gymkhanas. I didn't often make it, but she certainly didn't need me to help her go on winning the little cups.

Pete had got into motocross at the tender age of four, so I took home a miniature automatic 50cc Yamaha for him to try out in the field at the side of Station House. He took it round and seemed to be steering well, but when he realized he didn't know how to use the brakes he came to a sudden stop by crashing into a rock. We had to laugh, as he was unharmed, and I said, 'I think I'd better buy that for you, now you've broken the mudguard.'

I didn't get to see Pete win his motocross trophies in years to come either, because I usually spent Saturdays on the road. There was still a lot of work in the North, too, through a guy called Les Parker. Some of 'The Comedians' crowd were big stars and their money suddenly went up to telephone numbers. Though I wasn't a big star I didn't mind seeing people getting paid twice as much as me so long as there were no gaps in my diary. If the phone didn't ring for a week or I had a few blank days in the coming month, I would panic and want to start phoning around the country to look for work, but Phyllis never seemed to worry, or at least she told me not to worry.

'Something will turn up, it always does,' she'd say, when she saw me peering at the gaps on the calendar and, touch wood, she's always been right, although the late 70s were the leanest years by far.

As is often the way during difficult times, I made some significant friendships. Some of my best hard times were had at the Ram and Teasel, a little pub in Islington, which is where I met the inimitable Butch Royal and, through him, Ron and Marje, who have all become dear friends and sometimes let me tempt them away from the smoke to spend holidays with us. Butch has an exceptionally fine singing voice which has been known to reduce women to jelly in two bars. His off-stage penchant for unmatching pairs of illustrated socks and a tendency to fill pauses in conversation with imitations of a ringing telephone or by deftly combing his fringe (which once belonged to someone else) add to his lovely rapport with East End landlords.

Often Butch used his charm to help me find work in London. If I had a week with no bookings, I'd drive from Burton in Kendal down to Islington, meet him in the Ram and Teasel, and then go and watch him work. More often than not he knew of someone who could get me a gig and he helped me through the lean times, along with a few other gentlemen including the great London comic Jimmy Jones.

Not many entertainers are willing to take the risk of giving away their overtime, but working with Butch gave me a lot of contacts for which I was most grateful. Sometimes Butch would even let me take his gigs.

'Go in there at five minutes to nine,' he said. 'Tell them I've got flu, then they're unlikely to turn you down. I've got too much on tonight anyway, so my voice could well be fluey by nine o'clock.'

In the 70s you could still rely on a live backing band, with keyboards, bass and drums, and that helped a helluva lot if I needed to sing. On a really good night I'd find the courage to take my trumpet out of its case. If not for Butch I might never have experienced some of London's most prestigious venues, such as the Starlight Rooms in Enfield, the Green Man and the Dun Cow on the Old Kent Road.

Ah yes, and there were a few tricky evenings in Tottenham

at that interesting venue called the Eagle. At that time it was run by some rather shady gentlemen who were eventually taken away from society for a while, but they took a shine to me and enjoyed a good laugh, particularly with Butch. (Butch is unable to laugh properly without the help of a large white handkerchief to dab his eyes. It's a family trait inherited by his son and if you get the two of them laughing together enough eye-dabbing goes on to get the whole room reaching for the Kleenex.) But back to the Eagle. I remember going there one night when Spurs were playing at home and there was no one in the building.

'Well, there's nobody in,' I said. 'I don't suppose you'll be needing me tonight, after all.'

'Will you go on for us anyway?' said the barman. 'Because we like you.'

So the staff walked round the bar to stand with Butch at the back of the room and I did the act to four or five people. That night at the Eagle came to mind some years later when I had a horrendous night in York.

The Holgate working men's club in York had booked me for two spots and the first one felt as if I was in intensive care for twenty minutes. Towards the end of the spot I seemed to pass away. The microphones were pre-Edison and the keyboard player wore boxing gloves, but apart from that everything was completely my fault. My half-hour performance was pathetic, but they had made the mistake of paying me before I went on, so when I came off there seemed absolutely no point in going back on again. I gave my driver the nod and we crept out to the car. Two big committee men followed me out of the club, stood in front of the car and said, 'Right, give us half the money back.'

'It was £70,' I mused. 'Can I keep forty – a fiver for petrol?'

They said, 'No. you take £35 and if you don't give us the rest back we'll take it out of your face.'

Nice cathedral-city parlance, that, I thought. I would have quite enjoyed being back in Tottenham. I've never forgotten or forgiven that club in York.

Another memorable grimace spot was at South Shields British Legion Club for Sunday lunch. There was always a stripper on and she was usually a model for either *Farmer's Weekly* or *Exchange & Mart*. As I walked on to do the spot I looked out at the assembled South Shielders and the first thing that I saw was three tables pushed together in a line right in front of the stage, with eight men sitting alongside each other, elbow to elbow, pint to pint, directly facing the stage and doing a good imitation of a jury bench.

I was doing a forty-minute spot, and every two minutes one of these eight guys would stand up, walk across the front of the other seven and go to the bar to bring back one pint of beer. At two-minute intervals this went on right through my forty minutes, because over forty minutes eight fellas can drink about three pints apiece. But all through this, none of them laughed. They all sat there frosty-faced right through the whole of my act.

I did okay with the rest of the room but, as any performer will tell you, you become obsessed with the ones who are not laughing. Anyway I wasn't too ill and I got away with it, which is saying something in the north-east. I came off to applause, excepting of course from the eight poker faces at the front from whom there was no reaction whatsoever, and went to the bar. One of the poker faces came over to me and said, 'Why, you were great, Jim. We thoroughly enjoyed ya.'

I said, 'Well, why didn't you tell your face you enjoyed it? Why didn't you laugh?'

'Well,' he said, 'the eight of us have a bet every Sunday: the first one of us to laugh at the comic buys the other seven a drink.'

How's that for a challenge to a comedian? Thank you South Shields. Next time you enjoy yourselves up there, tell your faces.

18

My Athletic Phase

I never really understood how I was chosen to represent Charlton Athletic soccer team in 1979, but I was very happy to do my best for them in 'Up for the Cup', a new television series devised by ATV.

A dear friend, Ray Donne, Entertainments Manager at the Charlton Athletic Social Club, phoned and asked me to take part in the show: 'I'd like you to represent Charlton Athletic in a new TV series.'

'Nice of you to think of me, Ray.' I laughed. He had to be joking.

'It's a competition where different football clubs field entertainers to compete against each other . . .' Ray explained.

'It sounds like a talent show,' I said. 'I don't do talent shows. And how can you have a Lancashire comedian representing East London . . .? What time do you want me and where?'

Ray convinced me that doing the television series was a good idea, and he went on to act as my agent throughout 'Up for the Cup', 'Starburst', and the first series of 'Bullseye', after which he went into catering in Kent and I proceeded to look after my own affairs, which I have done ever since with the help of Phyllis.

'Up for the Cup' turned out to be great fun. It was conceived as a vehicle for displaying new talent at the same time as promoting soccer. Each football team submitted a team of entertainers to compete against each other. Bobby Davro was also 'playing' for Charlton and he shone like a beacon. Each team also had a 'joker', an act worth double marks, and I was Charlton's joker every week. We got right through to the final and we were eventually beaten by Manchester City.

I may not have known a lot about Charlton Athletic before the programme, but by the time we got through the first round I was rooting for them as wholeheartedly as their biggest fan, partly because I had a very good time making the show and partly because the more we went on winning the more I got to appear on television. So I was waving my rattle in delight when Charlton got through to the final.

I was also delighted to have been able to work with Albert Stevenson, the producer of 'Up for the Cup' who had also worked on 'New Faces'. When I went along to the recording studios and met Albert Stevenson, I quickly discovered him to be a very talented and charming man who knew show-business inside out.

Albert also had a lovely, dry sense of humour. He was once doing an after-dinner speech for a rotary club and the chap who introduced him mentioned the fact that Albert had been a prisoner of war in a Japanese concentration camp for six years. Albert went on to give one of his very entertaining speeches about the exciting world of television, liberally sprinkled with his clever, sharp wit. When he'd finished he asked the other guests, as is customary, if there were any questions. As anyone who has ever given an after-dinner speech knows, when the time comes for questions, you have to be prepared for the occasional yeuch one that threatens to dampen the convivial atmosphere you have just been nurturing and is usually offered by some smartie who likes to hear the sound of his own voice trying to appear serious after a bottle of claret.

'Mr Stevenson,' began the yeuch questioner. 'Can you please tell us, what was it like in the concentration camp?'

'For the first two weeks it pissed down with rain,' was Albert's priceless reply.

That was Albert all over, and that is exactly why it was a privilege to work with him.

At one of the recordings of 'Up for the Cup' I encountered the director Jon Scoffield, aka Scoff or The Immaculate Fridge because of the chilling effect he could create by simply walking into a room. It was said that Scoffield sacked Shirley Bassey and Bill Cosby for being too 'big time'. Jon wouldn't mind my remarking that he sometimes used to like a glass of wine and I'm happy to say that, although he never lost his dignity and poise, his manner was less chilly than usual when he knocked on my dressing room door as we finished 'Up for the Cup'.

'Do you know who I am?' he demanded.

'Yes, you're Head of Light Entertainment,' I said, thinking he probably didn't need to be told that.

'Right!' Scoff laughed. 'You're a funny man. I'm going to make you a star.' And with that he strode off down the corridor.

That night I went home to Phyllis and told her, 'Something very funny happened to me after the show tonight. You're not going to believe this, but the Head of Light Entertainment knocked on my dressing room door at the end of a long day and said he was going to make me a star! He seemed totally in control, but he'll probably forget all about it tomorrow.'

So I let the incident slip from my mind until I bumped into Jon again, three months later, when I was recording a 'Starburst' programme.

One of the funniest men in Britain, Norman Collier, was in the same programme. I was watching him doing his windscreen sketch in rehearsal and I thought, 'Oh my god, I'm next. I've got to follow that.'

Jon Scoffield appeared at my side, looked at my face, saw that my bottle had gone a little bit and said, 'Do we have a technical problem following Mr Collier?'

'Er, I'll go on where you tell me, Jon.' But Scoff moved me

to another spot, because he sensed in that particular instance my confidence might have been a bit low.

Later I was eating with a very funny ventriloquist called Neville King in the staff restaurant at Elstree when Jon Scoffield walked across the room, pointed at me and gave me a knowing nod. I knew then that he hadn't forgotten his promise to me.

'Up for the Cup', 'Starburst' and an autumn series of 'The Comedians', all in 1979, gave me just the amount of television I needed to begin to do justice to a new home, so this was the year we bought Station House. It wasn't exactly a house when we bought it and has been my main hobby ever since. You could say that a horse called Twinkle led us here . . .

Sue took her riding lessons in an interesting setting at the edge of the village of Arkholme. Her instructor Violet was the daughter of Margaret and Jack Alston, who lived in half of an old railway station, with enough land beside the railway lines to keep horses, give lessons and run a smallholding. When she was about two Sue took such a shine to a young foal called Twinkle that we decided to let her look after the horse at home, as we had a sufficiently large piece of land. The following year both Sue and the foal were big enough to start riding lessons proper and Twinkle became the love of my daughter's life. They were the same age and grew up together.

Twinkle is twenty-three at the time of writing and still teaching children to ride. I honestly don't recall ever paying Jack and Margaret for her, it was just one of those friendly set-ups with the stables. But Twinkle was to lead us to a far larger investment in the form of seven acres of land and a Victorian railway station.

I was standing watching Sue finish her lesson one day and got into a conversation about the house with Margaret. She and Jack had lived there since 1966, when they had bought it after the Beeching cuts because they wanted to use the land. For not a lot of money they got a 100-foot-long Victorian building set in seven acres.

'The part we live in was the stationmaster's house,' Margaret explained, 'But we don't really need the rest of the building. We really bought it for the land and put most of our energy into the smallholding.'

'What was the rest of it used for when it was a working station?' I asked her.

She pointed out the different sections along the building: 'There's the waiting room, the porter's room, the lamp room and the ticket office . . .'

My imagination was working overtime. As I stood talking to Margaret my eyes drifted over the view from the paddock of the house, the railway bank, the mason's yard and the smallholding. It was a higgledy-piggledy set-up, but I suddenly saw a great deal of potential and was gripped by the idea of living in a station. At that stage I didn't picture the Bentleys in the drive, but it seemed like a great place to develop a family home – a potentially large house with a little history attached to it and plenty of land that would make it an ideal place for the children. So I found myself saying, 'If ever you're interested in selling this, will you let me know?'

'Well, if you are interested, Jim, now's the time. You know what Jack's like – everything's for sale around here,' said Margaret.

'How much do you want for it?'

She named her price and I said, 'Okay, we'll have it.'

Then Margaret just went to the telephone and called her husband to say, 'I've sold the place, Jack, like we said . . . the agreed figure.'

And Jack replied, 'Oh, right oh!' And it was as simple as that – which has to be the best way to do business.

When the word got out that Station House was for sale Jack was offered a lot more money, but he wouldn't sell it to anyone else because he'd promised it to me and he held it for us for about seven months while a local businessman was making him a better offer every week.

'I've said Jim can have it and he can have it,' he'd say. What a test of honour. Jack was a different character but a man of his word. It's the only major financial step I've ever taken in my life without discussing it with Phyllis, who was leaning on the car bonnet while the conversation was going on with Margaret, so I presumed she would intervene if she had any objections.

'With a building as big as this one, whatever state it's in, eventually all that space has to make a nice house,' I reasoned. 'Given time, a successful television series, a following wind and good health, we can have a superb home, including passing trains. And neither of us needs to be an architect.'

Fortunately Phyllis agreed, but when we told Sue on the way home in the car she burst into tears because we were leaving a nice house in a village on the other side of the hill.

'I don't want to move from "Underfell",' she wailed.

Sue has since quoted my response to her insecurities as, 'Oh shut up and don't be silly. You'll enjoy living in a railway station.' She says she simply couldn't imagine at the time how the place could be a home. But if we left Station House now, fifteen years and fifteen stages of rebuilding later, our children would disown us.

And I think Phyllis might banish me to the caravan for life if I contemplated any more rebuilding, although I can still persuade her to agree to the odd seasonal adjustment in the grounds.

One of the worst decisions I ever made was during our first month at Station House. It simply involved saying the words, 'Okay, yes. Dad can come and live with us.'

My father's doctor had told me, 'He's not fit to stay on his own. He shouldn't be left alone now, so I suggest that he goes home with you.'

I should have been harder to be kinder to my father and said, 'Sorry, there's no suitable room for him. My wife is not trained in nursing and I certainly can't cope and Dad would prefer to go into a home.' Then a place would have been found for him and we would all have been happier.

My own doctor met Dad and said to me, 'You shouldn't have done that, Jim.'

I learned the hard way that trying to look after an ill eighty-five-year-old person is a road to catastrophe, especially if that eighty-five-year-old happens to be my father. Not that he was difficult, but he was eighty-five and, quite naturally, frail. And if there's any aspect of the relationship that can be preserved in such circumstances, it is best preserved in an old people's home where the staff are trained to look after old people, to move them more comfortably, to deal with their problems more efficiently and even fill their lives with more affection.

We didn't have a downstairs bedroom, so we had to push Dad up the stairs and get him into a position where he could bang on the floor if he needed Phyllis, as I was out working most evenings as usual. With Dad up there Phyllis certainly couldn't bring two children up and look after me. The demands were just too great, although, of course, Phyllis would always try the impossible before believing it was impossible.

One day Dad made his own way downstairs and announced, 'I'd like to see Sue have a ride on her pony.'

It was pouring with rain. Sue went out to brush the pony, got dressed up in all her gear and we drove him up the garden to a place where he could look down on the paddock. Sue was riding away, drenched to the skin and doing her best to look as if she was having a great time and it was the most normal thing in the world to go riding in a storm if your grandfather was watching. But he wasn't!

When I walked back to the car he was engrossed in the newspaper. I knocked on the window and said, 'I thought you wanted to watch Sue. She's out there, look, riding so you can watch her.'

'Oh no,' said Dad. 'I'm all right reading the paper.'

'Well, perhaps you can read the paper indoors, then Sue can dry out?'

That's what it was like, frustrating for everybody. So we did our best to get Dad everywhere he wanted to be, which was primarily in an old people's home back in Clayton-le-

Moors where he felt comfortable and knew people. There was just the little problem of the fastenings to get over, because when we had found a place in a home the matron said that Dad should be able to 'do for himself'.

'In what way, especially?' I enquired hesitantly.

'Oh, you know, dressing himself and things like that, all the fastenings,' said the matron in an optimistic sort of way. 'Can you bring him down next week?'

'Yes, thank you,' I said and considered the matter settled.

Dad was quite a well-fastened kind of guy on the whole, except by now he was beginning to look a bit unfastened because his clothes and spectacles had the habit of settling at strange angles while he remained absolutely dignified in himself for most of the time.

The day we set off to drive to the home was a good day for Dad. Everything was fastened and he seemed happy at the prospect of the trip.

'When we get to the home, we need to turn left so we don't park in front of the matron's office,' I said to my driver Pete.

The driveway took us by surprise and Pete turned right and stopped bang in front of the window of the matron's office.

I didn't really want the matron to see Dad getting out of the car because, although he had been well fastened together when we'd set off, there was no knowing in what manner he could be got out of the back of the car, how long it would take, or what degree of unfastening the activity might lead to.

The only thing for me to do was to get out of the car and wave wildly at the matron's window to attract her attention while Pete manoeuvred Dad, a skill in which he had already proved himself particularly adept. So Pete got out of the car behind me and pulled Dad out of the back seat like a ventriloquist's dummy and held him upright.

'He's all right, matron. He's coming round to see you now.' I gesticulated at the window.

Pete was carrying Dad in an upright position. Although

his feet were not touching the ground, Dad was doing a very good impression of walking across the tarmac and by the time we got him into the foyer he was able to stand. I put his hat back on and straightened his glasses.

'I'm having a bad day,' he said.

'No you're not, Dad,' I said. 'You're having a good day, for the next ten minutes you're having a very good day.'

We knocked on the door and shuffled him in and got him sitting on a chair.

'How are you today, Joe?' asked the matron.

I said, 'He's very well.'

She said, 'Can you do yourself up and everything, Joe?'

'Look at him,' I said. 'You got yourself ready today, didn't you, Dad? All the fastenings fastened up, eh?'

'I just have a bit of a . . .' Dad began.

'He's no problem,' I interrupted. I wouldn't let Dad say a word. 'He's so pleased about this, because he really wants to be near his friends in Clayton.'

'That's fine then, Joe,' said the matron. 'You can come in next week and we'll have a room for you.'

'Ooh, er . . . Oooh,' I said. 'We can't wait until then. I've got to go straight to London. Have you got a broom cupboard you could prop him up in or something?'

The whole scenario very much resembled a dialogue between Hilda Baker and her slim, dumb friend – a 'She knows you know' sketch if ever there was one.

Fortunately the matron was very understanding and it was an excellent old people's home. I'd arranged with my driver that if the home had refused to take Dad, I would run out and he should be ready to start the car and leave him. That was not callous; by this time I knew that the most caring thing I could do for Dad was to get him into this home, the place where he wanted to be. He felt safe again in Clayton-le-Moors, where he had spent the whole of his life. I firmly believe that there should be no pressure from the health services for people to look after elderly relatives at home. Of course, some people can do it well and want to do it, but most of us can't and don't have the necessary experience. It's very much a personal thing and I'm probably being dogmatic about it, because I learned from my mistakes.

Dad died in 1979, when he was eighty-six, and I think he died because he just wore out and that's not a bad shelf life. He caught a cold and his system wasn't strong enough to take it; it was sad, but not nearly as sad as many losses suffered by other families.

He had enjoyed brilliant health and had never been sick before, so he wasn't very good at being ill. I know how to be sick and I'm very bad at it because I find that helps me get better. It's all right saying I wouldn't mind being given a chit to say I can live until I'm eighty-eight, but when I got to eighty-seven I might begin to regret having settled for that chit.

My father and I hadn't exactly resolved our differences before he died; we had rather grown to accept them and along with that the recognition that we didn't want to be part of each other's lives. This sounds very heartless when written down in black and white, yet that is honestly what I feel. Dad had accepted me as a baby with squinty eyes, diphtheria and all the uncertainty of an unknown medical history, so when I'd made a success of my life in his terms I suppose I felt he should accept me as an adult and be proud of the fact that I had a good marriage that had given him two lovely grand-children. I never featured in his hit parade either and he took solace in his friends. His visits became less and less frequent and he was in good shape until his late seventies.

I once heard from a friend of Dad's how he talked about what Sue and Pete had been up to and how proud of them he was, but, sadly for everybody, he never let them know, he never showed it to their faces. He was never the kind of grandfather the children would run and meet with open arms. But, after all, I'm not really that kind of father either.

The great sadness is that I simply cannot recall any time when Dad showed affection. Having watched my own son grow up, I can look back to my childhood and see times when

I really hurt my dad and he would refuse to acknowledge the fact. His generation of men led an industrious life with little time or inclination to express their feelings. The breadwinner's energy for work was his *raison d'être*. Work was more than a major part of Dad's identity, his work was synonymous with his identity, and when he retired all that was left was a brick wall between him and the world of emotions. He seemed satisfied to watch the world go by from behind his brick wall, with me and my family forming no part of his universe. By the time I got married I too had absolutely no desire to do battle to keep the communication lines open; I was busy getting on with my own life and my father made it crystal clear to me that he wanted no part of it.

The brick wall began to crumble somewhat when Dad reached his seventies. He began to lean on me a little and we had got over our lack of communication problem by simply not expecting any praise from each other. On that note I'm willing to accept that it was more or less all my fault – I wanted from him what he could not give and wanted him to ask of me what he did not want.

It seems to me that the influence of grandparents, even in their absence, will always act as a subtle and positive counterpoint to the best efforts of their own children. The first present Sue ever had was a cuddly teddy bear from her uncuddly grandfather. I'd like you to know, Dad, that your bear has been loved so much that it has metamorphosized into a long, thin hairless object that resembles ET and has travelled the world to watch over your granddaughter's dreams in twenty different countries.

19

Station House

When we first moved to Station House Phyllis took over the running of the riding school for a few years, using the little booking hall as the tack room. Sue's riding teacher Violet, the daughter of the previous owners, stayed on in a flat beside the tack room and worked as a riding instructor.

In the beginning we played about at living in the space, trying to work out the best way to use the rooms, because the house is only one room wide, so you don't have a choice of routes from A to B. It was like living in a long corridor, with the tack room at one end and the kitchen at the other, facing a derelict outbuilding that still housed a few hens. For about three months Pete made a good living selling eggs to the village shop, but one by one the hens died. I think it was because they were living on a diet of dog biscuits.

We gradually began working out the jigsaw that would turn a station into a home while keeping as much of the railway atmosphere as we could. As far as I remember, the kitchen has always been the kitchen, but all the other rooms in Station House have changed roles at least once.

It had been a busy station in the 50s and 60s, so there was a large area of hard standing where the wagons came down to pick up coal from the sidings. The surrounding land has been a joy to work on. There's a tree next to the tennis court that's even older than me and another tree died on us when we moved it to provide shelter for the summer house, but it was only warning us not to move any other trees, as it came back to life after two years and shot up. We've kept the wood store, where we keep the wood to dry out as a sort of secondary pension, which we have to tell everybody about when we sell it.

There's a spring running under the railway line where the sidings were which runs through to a neighbouring farm and caused a boggy patch that nothing much could be made of except a pond, so we brought in a digger and just dug and dug so the water came through and filled quite a lake, which gives a wonderful scenic view to my old lemon caravan. So now we have carp in what used to be a bog.

Since the children have grown up the land they used for horseriding and motorcycling has become redundant, so last year we planted a thousand Christmas trees in it, which we think will look rather nice if they survive and, of course, the village can have a Christmas tree whenever they want one.

The most recent addition to the garden has been new stone steps, which Phyllis thought totally unnecessary until the builder christened them our 'Fred Astaire and Ginger Rogers Stairway to Paradise' and suggested floodlights as a starry touch; the lights would add a certain grandeur when you hobbled down the steps at dusk, covered in mud after a long and satisfying day of gardening. I've never gone in for long and satisfying days of gardening myself, but our 'Astaire and Rogers' stairway does add enjoyment to walking out of the kitchen.

The first big re-building job we tackled was the garage, for which we used an existing outbuilding, moving it a foot and refacing the entrance. It's an outrageous size, but of course it was a British Rail warehouse at one time.

Then followed fifteen summers of living with a rent-a-crowd of renovators. The chaos didn't go away, it just moved around the building. We tried the main bedroom downstairs, then upstairs again, and have built into every available space of the original station, including the roof. The office found its place in the old waiting room; we moved a chimney, stone by stone, from one end of the house to the other; we managed an en-suite-cum-overhead bathroom on a platform above the bed; created a separate, very non-granny flat at one end of the house; installed a swimming pool at the other end; popped in a Turkish bath; and found a conservatory sympathetic to the style of the station platform, not too far away from the bar which was created out of a need to find a use for a very handsome pulpit rescued from a derelict Methodist church in Nelson, Lancashire.

To date I have only received one letter from a Methodist complaining about my profane use of a pulpit as a bar fitting. As I rescued the item from certain death and also stand in it to practice playing my trumpet, to which I was first introduced by the church, it seems to me a most happy arrangement. Funnily enough, it was pointed out to me by the expert carpenter that the ring mark on the inside ledge of the pulpit had burnt so far into the wood that it was far more likely to have been caused by regular drips from a whisky glass than by any innocent tumblers of Ribena.

I've enjoyed all the work we've done on Station House enormously, because I've been able to come back home from working weekends to see the place changing shape. By sheer coincidence I always seem to have been away when any major digging or building was going on. The week of the big mess would always find me at the other end of the country from where I would return to make happy noises about the finished work. Phyllis, on the other hand, has had to live with the dust and noise, and in our fourteenth year at Station House she put her foot down.

'No more building this summer, Jim,' she said. 'I'd like some time to enjoy the garden – and a house without gaps in – without the crowds of builders and clouds of dust.'

'I thought perhaps a little conservatory on platform one? It wouldn't be a major upheaval.'

'So we can relax there next summer?'

'Exactly.'

'No, thank you. I want to relax *this* summer. Do it when I'm not here.'

Consequently, Phyllis and Sue got to go to Egypt while I got to watch the builders and carpenters and enjoyed both radio one from the truck at one side of the house and jazz from the decorators' radio at the other as background music to writing this book. A decorator who can name Tab Hunter after two bars of *Young Love* is a rare find indeed.

After fourteen years of using the same builders, I would have missed their familiar faces and summer wouldn't be summer without the sunshine-yellow overalls worn by the little sunbeams from the window company.

I had to buy a mill in Halifax to get the stone to match the original building, and now we've used every available space. The railway track and Phyllis prevent any further developments; the house is finally complete and renovated. Oops, did I say finally? Well at least until I get a yen for a snooker room but I shouldn't mention that here, because if I so much as murmur about changing anything else in future, I'm sure to be faced with formidable family opposition.

We love living in the village and we've got a lot of respect for it. Station House wouldn't mean so much to us if we didn't have friendly faces nearby who've kept a quiet watch to make sure that their station wasn't being changed out of all recognition. The builders who have been with us since we bought Station House all those years ago – Bill Eglin, Robert Park, our very patient plumber Gordon Edmundson and the even more patient electrician Bernard Wills – all caring guys whose staff have given us a beautiful home – have worked with a lot of affection and care. The lovely thing is that if ever Phyllis is in trouble when I'm away on tour I know that she's only a phone call away from service and salvation.

We still get four or five trains a day passing each way and they seem to appreciate the work we've done on their old station because they always slow down and give us a pip on the hooter.

Only once has a train stopped at the platform. I heard it and rushed to the window to check.

'Phyllis, the 12.45 has just stopped right outside the house, on platform one.'

'Oh no it hasn't,' said Phyllis calmly, and stared into space with a slightly amused expression on her face.

'Yes it has ... it's the ruddy Flying Scotsman!'

I dashed outside to make sure I wasn't hallucinating and found a group of passengers had got off the train, and they all seemed to be walking towards me. I was still trying to work out what was happening when the driver, with a very grimy face, pushed through the little crowd and handed me a book. It was Eamonn Andrews and, as if that shock wasn't enough, I was then whisked off in a car to face a flight to London. We all had a fantastically memorable time on 'This Is Your Life', and the day proved to me that the greater the treat at the end of a flight, the easier it is to overcome my fear of planes.

20

'Bullseye' and the Bottle Factor

In September 1980 I received a telephone call at the Crest Hotel in Wrexham that changed my life. When the phone rang I was lying on the bed in my hotel room, anticipating nothing more than the evening ahead at Wrexham Football Club, where I was due to speak. I was looking forward to meeting Mike England, one of my idols when he played for Blackburn Rovers.

'Hello! Jim Bowen? This is Peter Harris. I'm a director at ATV,' said the glitzy voice on the phone.

I sat up sharply. A television director had found me in Wrexham!

'Jon Scoffield asked me to find you very quickly,' Peter Harris went on. 'Now, what exactly do you *do*, lovie?'

'I'm a comic,' I said, thinking that this call sounded very showbizzy. Give me more ...

'Look dahling, this is all rather embarrassing because I don't know who you are and we want you to host a game show. Would you be interested in meeting up?'

There was only one answer, 'Yes. What time do you want me and where?' This wasn't a moment to bother with a year-planner.

'Would you prefer Birmingham or Nottingham?'

'I'll meet you in Penzance if that's where you want me to be,' I told him, not wishing to appear anything less than as eager as a ferret in a trouser leg.

'Well let's say Birmingham, at the Grosvenor Hotel, Hagley Road. Would that be all right, my love?' said Peter.

It was more than all right. It was a day which I hoped would change my life. And it did.

I hadn't asked how to recognize Peter Harris, but it posed no problem. A sixth sense told me it was the man with luxuriant white hair, who was weighed down with gold. He wore a dozen rings, a diamond-studded watch, a solid gold Kermit the Frog on a chain round his neck, and a huge gold bracelet that I think he stole from a British Rail siding. It was certainly strong enough to pull coal trucks.

As we walked into the Grosvenor, someone said to him, 'Hello, love, I don't know whether to kiss you or weigh you in for scrap!'

We sat in the Grosvenor like the thorn and the rose, with a pint of beer and a glass of champagne in front of us, and as we spoke I quickly learned that Peter Harris is a gem, a lovely, lovely man, committed body and soul to being totally outrageous and totally professional. The golden Kermit is a memento of his days as director of 'The Muppet Show'.

Peter rattled his jewellery enthusiastically and explained his brief: 'You see we've got this game which should appeal to the pub-going members of the population . . .'

Plenty of them, I thought.

'It's based around darts players actually . . .'

Plenty of them, I thought.

'. . . And pub quizzes.'

Plenty of them, I thought, and said, 'Count me in, please. It can't fail.'

Super, smashing, great. Network television here I come.

Peter Harris gave an effervescent chuckle – I wasn't sure whether it was a response to me or to the champagne – and went on to point out that the programme was not to be modelled on any slick game show already established in the States. One of the important things about the game is that it was made in England. We hadn't inherited a successfully evolved American animal and given it a father, which had been the pattern for other successful game shows of the time such as 'Three, Two, One' and 'Family Fortunes'.

It turned out that I had been fourth on a short list of three to host what was to be 'Bullseye', but coincidences, fortunate ones for me, had eliminated the three preferred choices. One of them, a comedian from the Midlands, had needed to look in his diary when offered the opportunity by Peter, at which Peter Harris had flounced off and reported the episode to Scoffield, who said, 'Forget him, we'll offer it to Bowen.'

A comic in Birmingham now receives a diary every year as a gift from one grateful game-show host.

Peter Harris confirmed that I'd been noticed by Jon Scoffield in my couple of appearances in 'Starburst' at Elstree for ATV. I had been chosen to do the pilot because I was a northern comedian who had no preconceptions about how a game-show host should behave. Although Peter didn't say so, it was obvious that I was unlikely to turn a sow's ear into a silk purse.

We went into one of the function rooms at the Grosvenor to rehearse the programme, and there I met another impressive Peter. A man who has forgotten more about television than I will ever know, Peter Holmans represented the man who devised the game. He helped to set up Anglia Television and Yorkshire Television, and produced massive 60s shows like '$64,000 Question', 'The Sky's the Limit' and numerous other light entertainment and indeed heavy entertainment programmes.

In the presence of these two big potatoes, I decided that if they said it was Christmas, so be it. I think that's called career management. I knew I was going to host a game show, but as yet I had no idea how.

The concept was that the contestants threw darts at categories on a dartboard. It hadn't even reached the sow's ear stage, so we were starting almost from scratch and we all had to work on the idea together and develop it. We had to work out all the moves, the scoring standards, rules, and different sections of the game over a period of several weeks.

I arrived home at Station House in a state of high excitement and said to Phyllis, 'It looks as if I've got a chance of fronting what could be a very successful game show.' Even at this embryonic stage I had a gut feeling – my feelings are always in my stomach – that it was going to work: darts is a popular game; trivia is popular; put the two together and it had to be an extremely successful combination. With a following wind, I could see the big time in the distance.

We had been living in Station House for over a year by then, so we were no strangers to the Bay Horse, our local hostelry, but for a few weeks the licensees Norman and Kath came to regard me as part of the bar furniture. I spent every spare moment studying at the bar, talking about darts to anybody that would listen – and some that wouldn't – and jotting down numbers on beer mats. I used the Bay Horse as a centre of learning for the evening study of darts, planning the scoring strategy for the game and trying out various elements with the locals. The darts players were all much more knowledgeable than me and willingly experimented with different scoring possibilities. They knew they were helping to create a television series and they knew how much I wanted to make it work.

I must have mentioned it in every after-dinner speech I did that season. People still come up to me today and say, 'I remember when you spoke to us at the Cleckheaton Pigeon Fanciers do and you were just starting to make "Bullseye".'

'I've been asked to host a game show ... It could either make me a star or print me out a P45,' I told the Lune Valley Farmers' Club when I spoke at their dinner. I have given their after-dinner speech on several occasions since and my fee has always been a lovely brass calendar. I don't know how many I've got now but they are dotted all over the house and I look at them with great affection as among the best fees I've ever earned, because they are from people who are part of our lives at home.

Getting the game right was very much on my mind at all times. Whenever I went into a pub with a dartboard my eyes lit up and I'd soon be asking someone, 'Excuse me, can you score 101 with six darts? Now try 121 in six. Which is the more acceptable challenge?' One hundred was no good because that is five straight twenties, 121 didn't work either, and in the end the 101 score proved more feasible, so we went for that in the game.

For three months at the beginning of 1981 the 'Bullseye' team revised and rehearsed the format of the show. All the camera moves had to be sorted out by Harris P., the ever-increasing complexity of the movements involving the contestants and myself alongside shots of the dartboard, prizes and facial reactions that captured the overall chemistry of the game.

Whenever we met up to work on the idea, we couldn't leave it behind afterwards when we left the television studio, so at the end of the day the 'Bullseye' crew – captain Peter Holmans, staff captain Peter Harris, first officer Keith Lascelles, and crew supervisor Barbara Bradbury, with bosun Jim alongside – would often be found in Mr Chan's Chinese restaurant in Birmingham ruminating over the prawn balls about the show's growth and development.

'I think we should have a cheeky little cartoon character . . . a hairy bull, perhaps, called Bully from "Bullseye",' mused Harris P.

And I'm thinking, Does this man know what he's talking about? A bully? We'll have all these hairy sixteen-stone darts players chucking darts and where will the cartoon come into play?

But the Peters knew the business. Bully was a stroke of genius. The character became a fantastic success and has given the programme a special appeal to toddlers because they love Bully and I'm an also-ran as far as they're concerned. Bob Cousins came in as producer three years later and suggested we give the contestants a bendy toy Bully, and now I never travel anywhere without mine.

One of the big problems we discussed in Mr Chan's Chinese restaurant was the gamble, which was crucial to the pace of the game; it had to be an attractive gamble and we had to work out what we called the 'bottle factor'. We had learned that a good darts player could get 101 in the pub, but we had to consider how people could be expected to perform in a game situation. If you put darts players into teams and there's a prize to be won, even if it's only a fortnight in a hut in the Lebanon, an element of pressure comes in and performance deteriorates. To work out how much the bottle factor was going to affect performance when there were studio lights, an audience and prizes, we kept repeating the game in as many competitive situations as we could. Peter Harris came up to Arkholme and met Norman and Kath, mine hosts at the Bay Horse, to try out the game with the villagers. We also practised with some of the darts players among the sound boys and the camera crew down in the ATV social club.

About eight out of ten players will get 101 with six darts in a pub, but the years have proved that only three out of the same ten players will achieve it in the game. Put an excellent player in that highly competitive and alien situation and his performance suffers, because as nerves come into play with the knowledge that £5,000 could be at stake, the dartboard shrinks.

Quite by accident we created the best final two minutes of any game show that has ever been on the box, because all human frailty lies there. The camera captures greed, envy, nerve, generosity, and, of course, the bottle factor. The players can perform in the pub but can they do it on television? The viewer can look at a contestant and try to guess whether he can keep his nerve or whether his bottle has run back home.

When we felt we had the bottle factor sorted out, we still had to polish up the middle section, where we use the red and black sectors of the dartboard and the phrase, 'Keep out of the black and in the red. You get nothing in this game for two in a bed.' It was decided in the first series that if the player hit a black sector, not only did they not get a good prize but their grief was intensified by offering them, for instance, an empty packet of crisps or a contract to sweep the M6. After the first series this idea was dropped because there was nothing funny about losing a nineteen-inch colour television set!

The final section of the programme was also much discussed outside. One night, having worked on the show all day in the studio, Peter Harris and I were driving back to the Strathallan Hotel in his lime-green Rover and our conversation kept jumping back to the problems with that final segment. We knew that we had three pairs of contestants and that one pair was going to get a chance to gamble for the star prize. It suddenly occurred to one of us that they might not want to gamble.

'So what happens then?' wailed Harris P.

'We have no show,' I concluded. 'Why don't we bring the second couple back and see if they want to gamble what they've won?'

'And if they don't want to gamble, then we bring back the third couple. Eureka!' Harris P. hooted.

It was a small step for mankind but a definitive leap for 'Bullseye'. The final segment worked and we were ready to go into the studios to rehearse with a view to making a series.

Being involved in so much detail in the creation of a new game show from scratch was very exciting and a whole new world for me. By the time we got around to producing the programme, the game was the thing. Perhaps I should have focused more on developing new skills as a presenter – indeed many people were to suggest as much when they came to see the series.

We went into the studio on schedule to do a pilot show in April and the designer was let loose with almost £1.50 to spend on the makeshift set. John Lowe, an excellent darts player, looked around in obvious bewilderment at what he had got himself into. I remember an occasion when the whole room froze while we were rehearsing camera moves, a sure sign that Jon Scoffield was standing at the back.

The Refrigerator spoke: 'Don't have Jim floating around like that all day, he's camera fodder.'

Peter Harris was working out all the shots, but I had to know where I was going; we didn't want to shoot it like a football match. It wasn't like doing a stand-up comedy spot with a microphone and a band at my command; I was faced with cameras, board, darts, interviewing contestants, scoring, prizes, rules, and I had to remember about ninety cues. Harris would speak to me from behind the freesias (fresh daily) on his desk, 'Look, love, you're talking to this camera now, then when you move across here you're talking to camera three. Oh and please don't forget to glance into camera six on your way across to your question drum. Remember your viewers are out there, dahling!'

These disciplines were completely new to a fairly selfish stand-up comic who had previously had to think only of himself when performing. I was having great difficulty in coordinating the new skills I was learning and the more I tried to remember, the more I resembled a plastic robot in rehearsals, so I think Peter Harris sensed that a lot of harsh criticism would have destroyed me. I would follow his instructions but I never really sat down and learned all the moves, yet he never made me feel that I wasn't working hard enough. I thought I knew exactly what he meant, but I didn't. I still had a lot to learn.

I had thought that I could present a game show by standing in front of the camera and being a good stand-up comic, but on screen it was obvious that I wasn't even sure where the cameras were, let alone which one of the seven I should be looking at.

Peter encouraged me to be as relaxed and entertaining as I was in the bar at midnight, but when I watched the pilot I knew I was as flat and wilted as last night's lettuce sandwich. This was like asking me to drive the Flying Scotsman, when all I'd done was drive my own act and even that with some difficulty. Fortunately I didn't realize quite how bad I was.

We had given birth to a game animal with no manners. It still isn't a slick show, but the pilot wasn't even potty-trained. We had devised a game that people would be happy to play in their local on Thursday nights; however, it was not yet good television and we all knew it. But we also knew that we had created a game with great potential, which, in the hands of masters of programme making like Harris P. and Holmans P., Scoffield J. (and later Cousins R. and Liddington D.) had more than a fair chance of success.

Almost ten years later Peter Holmans admitted to me that he didn't want me for the show at the beginning and that the pilot had left him in an advanced state of anguish. Knowing Peter as I know him now, it's easy to understand that he thought that his game warranted a big star and that he would have much preferred a smooth performer. Yet he never gave me anything but encouragement, never made me feel unwanted, and because of that I have been able to learn so much from him.

It was Jon Scoffield who always said that the game was to be the star. He saw me as a comic with an image that suited the show, and I understood that my role was secondary to the game. I was there to oil the wheels.

Despite the patchy pilot, I still felt good about the game and we were given a transmission slot of Monday nights at seven o'clock, which is what is known in the trade as a protected slot. Between 'Crossroads' and 'Coronation Street' people stayed tuned to the same channel whatever was on, so this is a time the television company often chooses to put out new programmes to see how they hold the audience.

We made the first two programmes and the following morning was the meeting of the long table with Peter Harris Peter Holmans, Keith Lascelles (Senior Floor Manager), Barbara Bradbury (Programme PA), me and the Refrigerator

himself, Jon Scoffield. After we had watched the two programmes an atmosphere that exuded all the triumph of a
home goal settled over the room. The shows weren't as bad
as I thought they would be; they were worse.

'Well, what do you think of them?' asked Scoffield.

There was a lot of coughing, leg stretching and staring at
the table, then a silence that lasted about five years.

I muttered, 'Erm, I think we can probably get them better.'

'We can edit them up quite a bit,' offered Peter Harris
trying hard to sound enthusiastic.

'I can see that you're not happy with them,' said Peter
Holmans.

'What you're saying is that they're not good enough.'
Scoffield looked around the table then said quietly, 'Burn
them.'

In two words Scoffield wrote off well over £20,000 and
the first two 'Bullseyes' were never seen again. It was a brave
decision because Jon's neck was on the line and he had to
answer to the accountants. So we got back to work and made
thirteen more shows, with only marginally better results.

Sometimes it took an editor and a director eight hours to
edit a twenty-five-minute show. One show took twelve hours
to edit – I was so bad it took twelve hours to make twenty-five
minutes look presentable. And they never ever complained. If
I said something in the wrong place it could take half an
hour's editing to rectify that mistake. So I must have been
terrible.

'We'll know after the third week,' Peter Holmans pronounced. 'In the first week the viewers will watch to see what
the programme is like. In the second week a few will stay
with it, and by the third week we'll know just how many
viewers we've held.'

At the crew party after the recording of the last show Peter
Harris walked in looking subdued. I noticed his gold chains
weren't rattling as cheerfully as usual, and I could have sworn
the Kermit hanging around his neck had a golden tear in its
eye.

'Here's a nugget of news to get the party swinging,' he said to me. 'I've just heard that we won't be doing any more "Bullseye".'

I thought, Well that's it. The programmes will go out and that will be the end of the game. And probably the end of me.

It was a Monday evening in September 1981 when the first 'Bullseye' was shown on television. Phyllis and the children watched it with me at home in an increasingly uneasy silence. At the end of the programme I asked my wife, 'So what do you think, Phyllis?'

She just said, 'I think I'll go and put the kettle on.'

Over our cup of coffee she chose her words carefully: 'Well, I was surprised at how unlike yourself you appeared on the box,' she began, and went on to suggest that I had seemed distracted by the different elements of the show, too anxious to be able to project myself in the way I did when I only had to talk to an audience. She saw immediately that the game was a great one but that I had to do a lot of homework.

Phyllis is my best and most constructive critic. Stunned journalists panned us from every direction. The very best of the thirteen shows were shown first and they got hammered, they got the mallet. I developed a manic grin as I read scathing headlines on the television reviews in the morning papers and, although I had always been impressed by Terry Wogan on radio, the precision of his performance really came home to me when he announced that twenty-nine of my 'smashings' had been counted in twenty-four minutes. I had been completely unaware that I used the word so often and Terry reported it as an exceptional feat: 'Where will it end ... will Jim Bowen's vocabulary reach double figures?'

Another sharp-eye called me 'Colander Fingers' because every time a dart was thrown I used to walk up to the board and point to where it had landed. Although the nickname was quite amusing, at that point there were very good reasons for the finger routine: a lot of people don't play darts and like to see where the arrows land (that's why Tony Green always says the score after each dart) and we also have a lot of blind viewers who enjoy the programme and they want to know what the score is. We have tried to use Ceefax for the deaf, but we haven't managed to get that yet.

One evening shortly after the first 'Bullseye' was shown and the critics had so gleefully slammed it, I walked into the Midland Hotel in Morecambe, with the express wish of hiding in a corner behind my pint, because I just didn't feel like speaking to anyone. Who should I see but Eric Morecambe, who beamed over at me and made it seem like the most natural thing to do was to go and sit with him.

'I read the *Mirror* this morning,' he said as I sat down.

I groaned inwardly. So had I!

'Don't take it too badly, Jim. Just remember that yesterday's newspaper is the hardest thing to find in anyone's house.'

Eric's words made something click into place for me, like the last piece of a puzzle. That was the start of my learning to handle bad press. I'd never had to deal with it before, but I'd never done a game show before either.

I decided to read the papers without my glasses for at least three months, still feeling insecure in the knowledge that, with the best shows going out first, the worst was yet to come. Once again I started to consider situations vacant in the Church of England. The cassock seemed a viable option. But my career move was delayed by my gut feeling about the strength of the game and by the viewing figures.

By the third week the figures had dipped from eight to six million, then something strange and wonderful happened: they rose steadily to twelve million. I worked out my own theory, which was that people were watching 'Bullseye' because they couldn't believe how bad it was; they'd say, 'We'll watch it next week and see if it can possibly get worse again,' and as the weeks went by they were saying, 'This is incredible, you've got to be skilful to get worse than this!'

Millions of viewers found the programme's rough edges

endearing because they had seen nothing quite like it before, nothing quite so bad and no game show with such a gauche presenter who wasn't trying to prove himself. Ironically – and this particular irony was a joy to me – by the end of the series of thirteen programmes, viewing figures had put us in the top five most popular programmes. It's easy for me to emphasize the shortcomings and teething problems because I played a major part in them; 'Bullseye' was not a great show in 1981 and we all knew it, but it was a great *game* – the game was the thing. And the strength of the game shone through my ineptitude. Now I am slightly clearer, I hope that perhaps the game shines through even more brightly. But in 1981 we had made thirteen programmes that looked likely to set back the television industry by thirteen years.

Everyone seemed to want to kill it, but the viewers were telling us otherwise. So I nursed a strong feeling that there would be another series and an even stronger feeling that if I wanted to host it, I would have to improve my performance tenfold.

At the end of the run we had a second meeting of the long table with Jon Scoffield and this time there was only a three-year silence before he said, 'Congratulations everybody. You have made a series that has been in the top ten for thirteen weeks. We're doing another but you're coming off prime time and they're going to put you out on Sunday afternoons at four o'clock.' This sounded good from a man who never gave praise to anyone, then came, 'They're trying to bury us on Sundays. Now do you think we can get a game out of this bloody mess?'

Ouch! We'd been lifted up to be given one of Scoff's specialities – a perfectly timed kick in the balls.

21

Even More Super, Smashing

and Great

The first series of 'Bullseye' was something of a sow's ear, without a doubt. It wasn't even half a sow's ear. It's still not a silk purse after thirteen years, because it hasn't lost too much of its down-to-earth approach. I like to think I'm still the same guy who bungled his way through the first series. The difference now is that I turn up in a nicer car.

Jon Scoffield put his stamp firmly on the second series: 'Right, it's a game for losers at the moment, so we improve this, this and this and we up the prize money.'

In 'Bullseye' he saw the kernel of something that was a survivor. That's why he burned the first two shows and that's why he lived with it and fought for its life after the first series had gone out on Monday nights. The TV network wanted it off the box as quickly as possible but they couldn't ignore the fact that so many viewers were watching it. We had this game whose roots were with the pub-going members of the population and we felt we had started to win their loyalty.

Our spirits were up and Peter Harris's fresh freesias were back on his desk, but the idea of a Sunday spot was a bit daunting. On Sunday afternoon people are out doing their gardening at a quarter to five and it is also a time when a lot of people cook or put their heads in the oven when faced with the prospect of an hour of hymns, prayers and collars on back to front on television.

'Let's try and go out with a bang. With this second series we'll give 'em a decent game to say goodbye to,' said Scoff, who believed that the 1982 series would be the last because he'd had to put up such a fight to get us sixteen more shows.

ATV still saw fit to use me in 1982, as a stand-up comedian in 'Starburst', their variety spectacular transmitted at prime time on Wednesdays. When I heard that Bob Monkhouse was working in a nearby studio while I was recording a 'Starburst' down at Elstree, I took a deep breath and resolved to ask his advice.

'Bob, I really am struggling with this game-show host bit . . .'

He took me aside for twenty minutes and we had a good chat.

'Learn your cameras, Jim,' said Bob Monkhouse. 'That's the starting point, and you can't develop anything else until you know, without thinking, that camera four, for example, is going to be at forty-five degrees and you know that when you look at that camera the light is going to come on and you are going into people's living rooms through it.

'Get to know the camera moves by heart. Take them home, take them in the car, go to bed with them.' Bob is regarded by most people in the business as the ultimate professional. He has a fine mind and is a great thinker. He is certainly the best quiz-show host there is, a superb technician and a good timer of a line. On and off stage he is continually working and honing his skills. I've watched him work on an after-dinner speech and his technique and memory skills are superb. Bob prepares meticulously, memorizing the names of foremen and senior managers present at the function, even though he doesn't intend to use half of them. He's a stayer and he's still at the top. Yet many television viewers don't like him because he's *too* good. Isn't that amazing? We Brits sometimes don't like excellence.

Bob once said to me, 'You're a clever sod you are, Jim.

You make mistakes and people like you, and they hate me because I try and get it perfect.'

An example of Bob's attention to detail and diligence became very apparent at a dinner we were privileged to attend servicing Bob's favourite charity at the Hilton Hotel in London. Our dear friend Betty B. was thrilled to see Bob there along with other big stars. After the meal she plucked up courage to go to the top table with her autograph book.

'Excuse me, Mr Monkhouse, could I . . .'

'Don't call me Mr Monkhouse,' put in Bob with a big smile before Betty could finish her request. He made sure she was completely at ease before he signed his autograph, in fact she was so charmed that she told me she didn't sleep properly for a week.

Bob has decades of experience in almost every department of the entertainment industry. If a Martian met him face to face he would know he was in the presence of a star. And I was very grateful to him for making time to advise an elderly novice like me.

I realized I had to build on the best parts of 'Bullseye' and learn from my mistakes. I wanted the series to run and run, and I wanted to remain a part of it. Peter Harris had asked me if I wanted someone else to do the scoring or someone else to warm up the audience in the first series and, like a silly billock, I'd said no. Now I realize it would have been a big help to have someone to look after the audience while I was worrying about the contestants and to have someone else to deal with the confounded arithmetic of the scoring, which definitely took up too much of my overtaxed brain space. I should have thought it through and thought bigger, but I was getting £200 a show and I didn't have a 'star' mentality. I wanted to do all the odd jobs, and I think in a way this kept me in my place, as a front man who wasn't there to prove himself, within the context of 'Bullseye'.

Tony Green was one of the celebrity guests playing for charity in the first series. 'I could do the scoring of the darts competition,' he said to me at the end of the programme. 'So if you ever need a scorer will you think of me?'

And we did think of him. Greeny is a great darts player who can calculate scores at the speed of light, and he was invited back to help with the mathematical moments in the second series. A great asset to the programme, Greeny has done more and more to take that bit of weight off me so I was able to concentrate on the other elements of the game and the camera positions. Apart from that welcome change, the programme's format is still very much the same as it was thirteen years ago.

Despite Jon Scoffield's prediction that the Sunday slot would bring a big drop in the ratings, 'Bullseye' went from strength to strength, increasing its initial Sunday afternoon audience from seven million to consistently topping eleven million. How delighted I was that for once Jon was wrong. I was even more delighted for Jon, because in our hour of need he had been a rock.

As a result of fronting a successful game on television, I suppose people have begun to notice me a little.

I was beginning to earn a more than respectable income and all at Central Television, formerly ATV, were starting to believe in the longevity of 'Bullseye', so I indulged my passion for and interest in motor cars by buying my first Rolls-Royce in 1986. A friend of mine who is an expert in these vehicles, Pete Yates, went on a mission to scour the country for an exceptional example of a Rolls-Royce Shadow II. He found one in London, at the showroom of Laurence Kane, whose young son was a keen fan of Bully (we were then in our fifth series). When Pete told Laurence who the car was for, he gave, free of charge, the cherished number plate 77 JBP. I'm not sure whether he knew my wife was called Phyllis or saw that the 'P' after 'JB' could be interpreted in other ways.

Pete bought the car for me without my seeing it. As he drove it into the yard at Station House, Phyllis stood at the door watching. The Rolls was a beautiful metallic silver, with dark blue hide interior, and I glanced at my wife's face to see her reaction.

Phyllis looked at the car, looked at me and said, 'This is a sad moment.'

'What makes you say that, Phyllis?' I asked, as I sped to inspect the vehicle more closely.

'As far as cars are concerned, there's nowhere for you to go from here!' She laughed.

Phyllis accurately assessed the situation. She realized that, as a middle-aged game-show host, I still needed goals, and the Rolls meant one less to aim for. In fact, the continued success of 'Bullseye' and its attendant remunerations in the form of personal appearances, after-dinners and cabarets, enabled me to raise my sights in terms of later, more expensive models of fine cars.

Instead of playing golf and involving myself in the busy metropolitan showbiz scene, I devote a lot of my spare time and money to cars. Bentley, Toyota and BMW agents enjoy a good standard of living when they have my phone number. I like good cars because they are all about excellence and technological advancement. The craftsmanship, the smell of wood and leather, the hand-finishing, stitching, polishing, all make me aware of what is possible. The lifestyle I lead means I live in a car for many hours a week, so why not spend that time in the best? It's quite nice to have the best available.

When the great Bobby Moore died at the age of fifty-one, I suddenly realized how short life can be. As my dustbinman friend said, 'We're only here for a bloody weekend.' That great loss to the nation prompted me to buy a car I'd always dreamed of – the Bentley Turbo R. Broughtons of Cheltenham afforded me my dream and came up with a beautiful midnight blue Turbo R with cream upholstery. The bank account was dented, my pride was boosted and Lloyd Bowmaker Finance shares rose.

The success of the 'Bullseye' package is due to the fact that Jon Scoffield recognized its potential when everyone else was fighting through a fog. If the job had gone to the Archbishop of Canterbury or Eve Pollard or even Bob Monkhouse it wouldn't have been the same programme, but people would still have watched it because it's a very strong game. A couple of days after we changed the performance of the cartoon Bully and got him to snort in anger when a contestant made a bad mistake, I was approached with complaints. I was opening a tile shop in Lichfield and two of the customers spoke to me about the change in animation.

'You know when Bully comes on and snorts and that steam comes out of his nostrils?' asked a concerned woman with an eighteen-month-old baby.

'Yes,' I said, sensing that she didn't want to talk to me about tiles.

'Well, can you stop that please, because every time he does it my baby cries. He likes to watch for Bully coming on with the dictionary, but he gets frightened when Bully starts getting steaming angry.'

'Oh, we can't have that,' I said. 'I'll see what we can do about it.'

I phoned Peter Harris as soon as the tile shop was open enough for me to go home, told him the story of my encounter with the anxious mother, and added, 'Do you realize you have created a character that attracts eighteen-month-old viewers?'

'We'll have to stop him steaming then,' Harris responded. 'We'll make Bully more animated and make sure he never gets cross again if that's upsetting children.'

Chris Wroe, the animator, replaced the snorting moments with a sequence of Bully putting his hands over his eyes and cringing at the mistakes. From then on everything that Bully did was friendly.

A great chemistry has developed between the members of the 'Bullseye' team and we've now got such a rapport that the work is an absolute pleasure.

There have been many hairy moments in the thirteen years of shows, and some I remember all too clearly . . .

We don't get many contestants we don't like, but the man in one husband-and-wife team aroused so much ill feeling in the studio that you could have cut the atmosphere with a knife. The woman was very bright, and answering all the questions correctly. The man was a prize wassock.

'Get me a cup of coffee!' he'd say to his wife as if he were talking to a backward Labrador.

The couple played the game and won a lot of prizes, then he insisted on changing his jacket for the second half.

'I hate him,' whispered Greeny.

When they got to the last part of the game, I knew that the prize was a car.

'Do you want to gamble?' I asked.

'I think we've done very well . . .' began the lady.

He said, 'Shut up. We're gambling.'

Greeny was thrilled to bits because he was sure they wouldn't win. I have to say I would have been quite pleased to see them walk away with nothing, but we did feel sorry for the lady, principally because she had an Obliteratus of a husband.

They needed 101 and the lady couldn't throw darts. She just threw them anywhere and scored seventy-five. Her wassocky husband needed twenty-six to win the lot.

He threw a twenty, then a five, and with his last dart he didn't even look at the board. He just threw it. The dart bounced out and they lost everything. The saddest thing was that everyone in the audience cheered like mad, which had to be edited out because the television audience would have no way of knowing that the contestant was a prize tosser.

Another contestant who gave us a slight problem insisted on wearing a cap with an enormous peak which shaded his face completely. We pleaded with him to take it off but he said, 'No. I'm leaving my cap on. I always play darts in it and I don't see why I have to take it off now.'

The cameramen tried to get different angles, but it was impossible, so all the viewers saw was a figure that looked very much like a penguin, with darts coming from underneath a big cap. The contestant turned out to be a great character, but he just hadn't understood the problem.

Probably my most nerve-racking moment on 'Bullseye' was when I thought someone had had a heart attack. The guy had been looking more and more unsettled as he answered the questions and started shaking like mad, then suddenly slumped in his chair. Honestly, I've seen more fat on Lester Piggott's whip; he looked very frail indeed.

Greeny shouted, 'Stop!'

Before you read on, it's important to know that this story does have a happy ending.

'How far are we from the commercial break?' barked Bob the producer.

'Thirty seconds,' I said.

'Can somebody just prop him up until we get to the interval? Okay, nurse?'

The nurse was there in an instant to make sure he was propped up in a medically acceptable way for thirty seconds.

Throughout all this Denis, the director, was saying, 'We'd better stop the show. We can't have this.'

'Denis, can I have a word with you?' asked producer Bob, happy that the nurse knew her stuff and playing for time as a producer must when he's thinking, Oh ... there must be a way we can shoot round him and get to the commercial break, because he's not going to win now and we can get a shot of him earlier on when he's not shaking ... and we've got seventy grand down the pan if we stop this.

And you think stockbrokers are under pressure!

While they were discussing whether we could manage another thirty seconds, there was this crumpled wreckage sitting there, oblivious to the nurse's attentions.

Luckily the nurse quickly established that the contestant's tremors were not caused by a heart attack. The poor man enjoyed a drink and, as the studios are dry, he had gone the whole day without a drop. So it wasn't a heart attack at all; a couple of scotches and he would probably have gone on to win, because he was doing very well.

After the commercial break he was taken to hospital against his wishes, to be thoroughly monitored and was brought back to the hotel next morning, put into a car and taken home. As soon as he was inside his own front door, he gathered speed and made a beeline for his domestic bottle bank.

So here we are thirteen years into 'Bullseye'. People ask, 'How does he do it?' People ask, 'Why does he do it? Perhaps it keeps him out of the army?' I've got news for them. I'm not joining up. With apologies to Terry Seabrook for the last paragraph.

22

Dipping

As I entered my fifties, the gas bills were no longer a problem, Phyllis's wardrobe bill wasn't making a dent in the bank balance, so I decided on a grand gesture for Station House – a swimming pool, next to the kitchen, because Phyllis loves to swim. Pete was doing nicely at Lancaster Grammar School and Sue, having completed her first year at Durham University in the Chinese faculty, would be spending some of her summer holidays with us before going off to China, where she had elected to do her second year to study Chinese. I thought it would be a nice, easy summer in 1988. For anyone who hasn't installed a swimming pool, I can tell you that it's very simple – once you have got the money together and found a bit of space you just order one of those swimming pool kits. You get all the pipes and tiles, and a very interesting instruction booklet. The only thing you don't get from the shop is the hole in the ground and it has to be said that creating the hole for the water involves a lot of dust and dirt because it needs to be massive, at least twelve foot wider and longer than the finished gap for the water. So we just made sure we weren't at home for the period of excavation. There's another good thing about building a swimming pool: it gives you a very sensible reason for going away on a fortnight's holiday, and coming back to a giant black hole in your property.

We had a wing section of the old Station House – well, a long shed really – that we hadn't yet played with and I worked out that it could be rebuilt as a swimming pool without contravening any of the building by-laws. The size of the shed could be increased by ten per cent without planning permission, so we did a few sketches of one rectangle representing the pool inside another rectangle representing the ten per cent larger shed, and the builders got on with it. We decided not to use an architect because we wanted it to look like a railway station from the outside, with not a trace of the style of Florida or Bermuda or Butlin's Waterworld, and particularly no plastic trees unless they were indigenous to Lancashire. With my limited drawing skills and a steady ruler I modestly decided that without too much fuss I could manage a simple echo of the style of Station House by using four straight walls, a large hole in the middle and a lot of tiles.

The only thing I had overlooked in my drawing was the matter of morning light. Fortunately the builders were men of artistic sensibility. They patiently explained to me that it would be nice to have light coming in from both sides of the pool, so they suggested a couple of roundel windows from a barn, which inspired me to add two stained glass Lancashire roses to my drawing.

There were a few tense moments when the plumbers needed page eighteen of the instruction booklet while the tilers were kneeling on page thirty-nine and the usually patient stonemason was threatening to tear out a whole chapter, but after the earth from the hole had been removed things went at such a pace that I was drawn into the throng and spent a few days moving stones and lifting large sacks of concrete.

Our village neighbours were a little curious and not at all worried. They like to keep us on our environmental toes, but they knew we'd got all the right stone so they wouldn't notice anything much different from the original shed when the pool was finished. To everyone's delight the building was taking shape very much in keeping with the surroundings.

One evening after a hard day of tiling Phyllis and I paid a rare visit to a local hostelry. The chairman of the parish council came into the pub and said to me, 'That's a big old hole down at Station House, Jim.'

And I thought to myself, Ooh he's going to stop us here.

Anyway he said no more and I met him again some time later when the pool was almost finished. I have to say it looked the business, totally in context. The building enhanced the overall site because the boss had done it well, with matching roof slate.

'Er, I see you've finished the building,' said the parish councillor. 'By Jove, that's a fair old sheep dip is that.'

I sighed with relief as he went on to say, tongue in cheek, 'You're all right, because you know you don't need planning permission if it's an agricultural building.'

Out of respect for the parish council we drag a lamb chop through the pool every Christmas Day to justify the sheep dip.

That was my favourite kind of summer, with plenty of action, dirt and noise, all the family at home and eighteen cups of coffee at elevenses. Phyllis had grown superbly phlegmatic about matters of dust by this time, but since the pool episode she has curbed my plans for extensions.

The reason the building of the swimming pool holds so many memories for me is because I was to go over the events of the summer of '88 again and again in my mind looking for an emotional watershed or a warning of what was to follow.

My fifty-first summer brought with it a number of more complicated consequences which should be borne in mind by anyone over fifty who is considering a similar project. Oh, I've no regrets about the pool – it's lovely and wet, I've been in it at least three or four times, had my photograph taken in it, rolling back the cover for Phyllis is a useful form of exercise and it has been known to serve as a spare bedroom. But I do wish I'd never been inspired by page five of the instruction booklet to lurch around carrying large sacks of concrete. The completion of the pool precipitated my very personal and painful dip into what some might term the male menopause.

When the day came for Sue to set off for China, I drove her down to Manchester with Phyllis to catch the plane down to Gatwick, where Phyllis was to see Sue off on her flight to Beijing via all points east. I remember seeing Phyllis and Sue walking down the corridor to the aeroplane and I knew that Phyllis would be back home soon but Sue wouldn't. As I drove home the dip started. Beijing isn't really within my parameters, in fact Blackpool is only just there.

'Bye, Dad. I'll write with a phone number,' Sue had said, perfectly calm and composed and not at all embarrassed about having packed in her rucksack the eighteen-year-old tatty teddy that her granddad had given her.

I knew Sue would write, I knew she would work and play hard and make the most of this opportunity. Everything had gone according to plan, we'd had a lovely summer and this was one of the first crisp mornings of autumn, back-to-school weather. I was the proud father, sharing Sue's quiet excitement at the new world that awaited her ... until I watched her walk away across the airport tarmac. She suddenly looked so young, and I was engulfed by waves of emotion that retreated only to lock in a knot in my stomach. Logic told me that this was what every father has to go through at that moment, but no reasoning could stop the feeling of dark emptiness inside that betrayed the frozen smile on my face.

I walked back to the car wishing I had been able to get on the plane to Gatwick. While I wasn't consciously aware of a crisis, my body told me otherwise. As soon as I got back into the car my stomach felt as if it had been consigned to grinding the whole of the brass section of the Manchester Philharmonic Orchestra, but every time it had a go at the euphonium player it rejected him and promised me another grind as soon as I ate something. I felt a protuberance the size of a billiard ball. I imagined I had every possible disease of the stomach. Raw memories of my mother's terrible illness returned and I gave myself a few hours to live.

Back at home I slumped on to the couch, feeling that my life was no longer of any consequence and I hardly moved from there for two months except to go out to work. A permanent brooding fixture on the couch, I became a still, silent albatross emanating gloom the length and breadth of Station House.

After playing with my stomach for a few weeks I eventually went to our doctor. Pippa Hall – a rather over-jolly name for a doctor, I think – told me that my muscle wall was slightly damaged. She should have a griffin above her medical diploma; a marvellous listening doctor if ever there was one.

Pippa was the doctor who had to endure a hysterical telephone call from me in Leicester, two or three years earlier. I was getting ready to do a cabaret and as I walked out of the bathroom I got a nasty shock from a full-length mirror. Suddenly my legs looked abnormal. I rang the surgery and Pippa answered the phone.

'I think my legs are going very thin,' I told her.

Looking back at this I feel ashamed. Do I really want to see this in print?

Pippa asked me if I got any exercise and I told her how I walk to the bar regularly and close the car door energetically. 'Well, you don't have to have a degree in physiology to know that if you don't exercise your muscles lose their tone and your legs will go a bit thinner,' she told me.

I was grateful for her advice and didn't bother her again until this problem with my stomach.

'Have you lifted anything heavy recently?' she asked.

I thought for a moment. 'I suppose I moved a few stones in the summer.'

'Well, there's nothing to worry about, just don't lift hundredweight bags with your legs apart otherwise something will drop and it might not be what you want to lose.'

I was so down I didn't listen, so frightened I started sweating every time my stomach churned, which was most of the time.

One night I was in bed listening to the rain and was on such a downer that I was sure of only one thing in life and that was that I wouldn't be around next morning. Movement seemed difficult but necessary, so I staggered downstairs holding my stomach and, as I slumped on to the settee, I located what felt like a football protruding from the noisy orchestra pit that was my intestine. There was nothing to be done now except go for a walk. The amazing thing was that I had no pain at all in my stomach; it was all the trauma between the ears, the mental spaghetti. These were the reactions of a totally irrational man.

The rain was sheeting across the yard, it was a monsoon, a storm fit for King Lear. At three o'clock in the morning, oblivious to the driving rain and wearing only pyjamas, I walked through the puddles in my felt slippers, waded into the muddy field and said to myself, 'Look at your beautiful house, the car, the land, look at it all now. There's absolutely no justice because I'm not going to be here all that long to enjoy all these things we've worked so hard to achieve between us.'

How ridiculous, sloshing about in slippers, talking to myself, soaked to the skin – but possibly as good a treatment as any for stress. I went to the fence where Mindy the horse would always come and find me for a chat and a mint. The horse duly trotted over and stuck its head over the fence. I looked it straight in the eye and said, 'I've got this thing, and I know it is my sternum, but it's getting bigger and it's been getting bigger for years. A billiard ball yesterday, a football today. There's no justice, Mindy.' And the horse looked at me and just turned and walked away.

I thought, Even the ruddy horse won't listen to me, so I went back into the house, went upstairs and at least had the sense to lie on top of the bed because I was too wet and muddy to get under the sheets. Phyllis was asleep and when she's asleep it's like Madame Tussauds on half-day closing, so I just lay there to dry out without disturbing her. By the time Phyllis woke up at six o'clock the room was light and I was getting warmer. She opened her eyes to see steam rising from my body and mud and grass splattered across the duvet.

'Where have you been?' asked Phyllis.

'Oh, I had a walk out last night.'

'You went out in all that rain?'

'Yes.'

'Why?' Phyllis was composed.

'Oh, I just felt like a walk.'

'Didn't you take an umbrella?'

'No.'

'What did you do?'

'I just had a word with the horse. It walked away.'

And we left it at that.

Phyllis knew Mindy very well and it had not behaved out of character for many years, so she must have thought, I know Mindy is an intelligent animal. If Jim is talking to the horse and the horse isn't listening, it must be Jim that's not being sensible. So she just temporarily gave up on me and I came round, as she knew I would.

It was a big dipper that would take over four months to shake off completely and nothing could penetrate the empty shell that I had become – not the ever-patient Phyllis, not boisterous Pete, not a new swimming pool, not a new car, not my hating myself for being unbearable to live with. Eventually I dragged myself to Doctor David Thomas for a full medical examination. Doctor D. T. models for Oxfam shops and looks like a misplaced New Age traveller. He is the kindest, most sympathetic doctor and I would like to emphasize that he and Pippa Hall have done absolutely nothing to deserve me as a patient.

'Press anything, doctor, but don't press my stomach or you'll find something.'

He pressed everywhere.

'Did you find something, doctor?'

'Nothing.'

'You didn't press hard enough then.'

After a thorough pressing, Dr D. T. told me I had nothing to worry about and I plainly didn't believe him. In his New Age sort of way he remained unsurprised by my irrational behaviour, drew my attention to the insidious pressures of my line of work and gave me a few tablets which I later christened my gerbil pellets.

I thought the doctor was being dramatic about the pressures of work, but I had to consider his opinion. When I was thirty-five I could drive down to London and back in a night or do three gigs – Leeds, Sheffield and Wakefield – then get up next morning and go to school, no problem. When I hit fifty I had to accept that my lifestyle might be taking its toll. Perhaps nerve endings get a bit thinner, just like teeth and hair. The power of adrenalin held me together for a performance, but for the rest of the time I gave in. I was convinced there was something seriously wrong with me. I was a goner. And when I was gone I'd be no good at all to Phyllis, Pete and Sue. I'd think, Just how irrational can you be, Bowen, you've got Phyllis, son and daughter doing well, no worries about the next bill, brand-new sheep dip, Rolls-Royce ...' And there I was acting the morose gerbil, being a pain.

Knowing I was being irrational didn't help. I imagined I had every illness in the book. Should I have spent more time with my children? If my nerves had split ends would they ever work properly again? Would I ever have the energy to walk to the car, let alone play football?

In the evenings the discipline of work dredged up some energy and I never missed a booking. As soon as my name was called to go on stage, something went zap! I went into automatic. Ironically, people were saying I was excelling myself. 'That was great, Jim,' said Jack Sharpe after watching me one night at a social club in Basildon. 'I've never seen you work better.' That meant a lot to me, because Jack Sharpe knows the business, but all I could think of was finding the strength to start the car and get home and spend the next twenty-four hours on the moquette.

I just had to learn to live with middle age, while Phyllis seemed to be able to do everything – she can still sit cross-legged on a bar stool like a leprechaun with an advanced yoga certificate, and give her a fortnight and she'll train herself back up to competitive standards in swimming, tennis or badminton. Throughout all my time at the bottom of the pit, Phyllis still remained absolutely steady, predictable, thoroughly reliable, strong and consistent. She never once reproached me or said the obvious 'Pull yourself together.' She just knew that one way or the other things would come round. As usual, she was right.

I remember one night during the middle of my dip when I noticed that Phyllis seemed a bit down and I said, 'What's the matter with you today?' I was annoyed that she was feeling low as well as me. I, who had not spoken to her for three months, apart from 'yes', 'no thank you' and, 'no, I can't be bothered now.'

Phyllis said, 'You're annoyed with me just because I'm having a quiet twenty minutes!' I was in the middle of having a quiet ninety days, so I shut up then. It makes me cringe to remember how insensitive I was.

I knew that a lot of men have to cope with putting weight on, taking weight off, not being able to play soccer or jump as high to head a ball, losing hair, teeth, eyesight and less action from Mr Happy, but it didn't help me feel any better.

At the time of going to press I'm fifty-six. They say that you're middle-aged at fifty-six but I don't see many people of 112, so people in their middle fifties had better stop deceiving themselves. Listen to Uncle Jim – you're more than halfway through your shelf life. The reason I'm talking about all this is that if any fifty-year-old fellas or ladies find they go through a phase where, for no apparent reason, everything falls out of bed, take it from me that the phase does pass.

I have always needed something to look forward to. At the age of seven I would count the days to our Blackpool holidays and imagine the thrill of seeing the shows on Monday, Wednesday and Friday. By the time it got to Thursday there was only one more show to look forward to and I'd dip a little, even as a child. But after fifty years of little dips, they become more difficult to handle and this one was a plunge into an abyss by comparison to anything I'd experienced before. As an adult I felt I should be able to create things to look forward to, after all I had everything I'd ever wanted in life. I knew there were no answers for me in Durham Cathedral or a Buddhist temple. The answers were under my own feet; each step was a question and the next step was its answer. I knew if I stood still I would achieve nothing and yet any step felt impossible to take. For three months there was no light at the end of the tunnel.

What a lucky man I was to know only three months of depression when many people battle with it for years. I can remember the date, the time, every detail about the bright evening when I came out of that tunnel. The end of my depression seemed as illogical as its onset.

Phyllis and I had tickets to the Water Rats dinner in November and had planned to go with our friends Joan and Pete Yates. I'd always looked forward to it before, but when Pete arrived at our house in his dinner suit I was still in tracksuited horizontal gerbil mode. 'Pete, I really don't think I'm well enough to go down to London today,' I said. 'Do you mind driving Phyllis down with you and Joan?'

Phyllis just looked at me in disgust and said, 'I didn't hear that, Jim.'

Gerbil Jim was ensconced in the back of the Rolls (registration number 77 JBP and at this point I knew exactly what the 'P' stood for) and I spent a wordless journey as far as Corley services where a fast-food experience in Julie's Pantry changed my life. I hadn't eaten properly for weeks so I ordered chips and a giant hamburger with an allotment on the side in the hope that something would tempt my appetite. Phyllis, Joan and Pete watched in amazement as I stuffed the chips from the carton into the burger and ate the whole thing without a pause. The three onlookers went on staring at me, waiting to see the effect of this fast-food attack on my weakened digestive system. I hadn't felt the need to eat a proper meal for some considerable time.

We all left the service area without saying a word. Thank you Julie's Pantry, for as I walked back to the car I felt a huge weight had lifted off my shoulders. I can see no explanation for the healing powers of junk food, but that's how it was and to anyone reading this now and suffering from depression, I wish you a speedy hamburger, a wagging dog's tail, spring flowers, a walk through the park or whatever it is that may one day herald a turning point to lift the weight from your life.

The Water Rats dinner was delicious. I ate as normally as I ever do and – would you believe it – won the first prize in the raffle, which was a return flight for two with American Airlines to California. This elicited gales of laughter, because almost everyone in the room knew I was frightened of flying.

'Auction it off,' I whispered to the toastmaster when I walked up to collect the prize.

'Get off, you prat, take it,' he insisted in his toasty tones, pushing the envelope into my hand.

I walked back to our table mumbling, 'Now what can *I* do with these?'

Phyllis beckoned me to her side and said quietly, 'Just give the envelope to me, please. You can go and talk to the horse. I'll take the return tickets for two to California, thank you!'

Sue and her boyfriend took full advantage of the flights to LA and had a fabulous time, stopping over for a few days in Chicago with a police chief who was a friend of James Whale who was a friend of mine. He met them in a huge pan-technicon of a vehicle and they had a great time, so the tickets I won were put to good use, though sadly not by yours truly. Maybe one day.

The morning after the Water Rats ball, I knew I'd had a drink or six the night before, but I didn't dip. I held on to the moment at Julie's Pantry and started to nail down that albatross.

All this was a necessary part of my growing-up process. Some people grapple with the issues of mortality and baldness at the age of eighteen, but for me it was a thankfully brief mid-life crisis, except that in showbusiness if the public notice that Jim's feeling a bit fed up tonight, the next thing you know he's having a nervous breakdown and by the time it gets into the press you're in a cell with padded walls and a heavy lock on the door.

A couple of weeks after my reprieve at Julie's Pantry I fell for the oldest trick in the Hack's Guide to Confessions when, during an interview with a journalist at home, I mentioned that I was feeling back on form after the roughest few months of my life. The interviewer sympathized – depression, recession and obsession being everyday small talk to a jobbing journalist – and I even had my photograph taken with the empty gerbil pellet bottles. The interview was ostensibly for a story about 'Bullseye' which had been given a prime-time slot before the Queen's speech that Christmas, but I'd provided the newspaper with a much more interesting line. A journalist from a rival tabloid kindly phoned me that evening to warn me of the following day's headline: Bowen Zombie Horror: Drugs Keep TV 'Bullseye' Star Sane. I was described as 'gaunt, unshaven and shaking nervously' – two out of three, but I'd call it svelte with designer stubble, despite the photographs.

The article appeared on the front page of a tabloid on the Saturday morning. The impression given was that I'd had a nervous breakdown, which simply wasn't true. I was appearing in Driffield that night and the venue was besieged with phone calls from ticket-holders who wanted to cancel that evening's booking, and they had to be reassured that I was not without marbles and would be appearing that night. I also lost three New Year gigs because people wondered if I was up to it, but the worst part was feeling such a fraud when I received hundreds of letters from concerned fans, some of them far more seriously ill than I have ever been.

Journalists tend to forget that if you report a piece in a certain way about someone who appears regularly on television, apart from the embarrassment and grief to the subject, it can also upset viewers. People watch 'Bullseye' for an anaesthetic, to get away from their troubles and it certainly wasn't my intention to appear in a national newspaper telling them about my little dip. I have always believed in the freedom of the press and fortunately this little episode did not change that opinion, for a few years later when a real problem rocked my homelife, I was to be grateful for the power of honest reporting.

The reaction from the village to the zombie episode was interesting; the village shop sold out of the newspaper in minutes, but when I went in the pub on the Monday night the regulars had cut out the pictures of me and stuck them all over the pub. It was a huge laugh, which I appreciated. People in the village hadn't been too aware I'd had a problem and they were pleased to see me up and about and kicking.

23

China's a Long Way Off

On 4 June 1989 I was compèring at the London Palladium with Jim Davidson at a spectacular charity performance in aid of the Sharon Allen Leukemia Trust (SALT). In the ten o'clock interval a late newspaper headline caught my eye that read '2,000 Students Killed in Tiananmen Square'. That was in Beijing. Sue was in Beijing, at the university, with the students, studying Chinese. There was no time to read the article because I was due back on stage. In the seconds that it took me to walk back out in front of that fantastic Palladium audience I had to dismiss thoughts of any China crisis. It was one of those moments when the wide world invades your heart and fights with common sense to tug at the emergency cord.

I had no idea of the total number of students in Beijing, I only knew that my daughter was one of them and my thoughts raced through a labyrinth of possibilities and priorities. If anything is the matter with Sue or Pete or Phyllis, I don't care where I am, I don't care if I'm top of the bill at Caesar's Palace, I want to go home! I'd taught my children to consider their priorities, to be true to themselves, and the knowledge that my daughter was a student in a city at the other side of the world where thousands of students had just been killed threw me into a feeling of total inadequacy. Sod the Palladium, unplug the microphone, start the car, what can I do to make sure Sue is okay? Of course, I didn't unplug the microphone; I pulled myself together, heaved my thoughts the 18,000 miles from Beijing and made my way back to my hotel to phone Phyllis at home.

Looking out of the car on the drive back to the hotel the London streets seemed to be teeming with twenty-year-old girls with dark hair and happy smiles who I wanted to be Sue. Two thousand young people had died that day; the whole world was shocked, but the whole world hadn't proudly encouraged their daughter to leave a quiet Lancashire village to study a culture so different from ours that this atrocity could happen there. But we hadn't raised the kind of daughter who was going to spend her life riding her horse around the paddock; we'd reared a globetrotter and I knew that China was only the beginning of her journeys, so I would just have to stop fearing the worst.

I phoned Phyllis from the hotel and she said, 'I'm watching Sky News and there's a report from Tiananmen Square every twenty minutes. I've phoned Durham University and they are in contact with Beijing. All the parents of the Durham students in Beijing are phoning round as soon as anyone hears anything, so there's nothing we can do but wait.' The phone didn't ring that night and I made no calls. It was a case of no news is good news.

Logic told me that Sue had no reason to be anywhere near the student demonstration, while fear told me that if she was inquisitive enough to want to learn such a difficult language she may have been drawn towards the square to witness the actions of her fellow students. She had spoken to us on the telephone only days before, saying that she and her friends had been sitting drinking tea with armed soldiers in Tiananmen Square. Now, however, it would seem the situation had dramatically changed and we could only hope that she was far enough away from this appalling scenario.

At two o'clock in the morning a journalist telephoned Phyllis to say that they had located Sue, safely asleep at Beijing university. Unusually, we didn't ask for your name, but to that journalist – thanks, I owe you a pint.

Mercifully, the phone rang in my hotel room in the early hours: 'The *Sun* has got through to Sue on campus by telephone. She's fine, she's in the campus outside the city . . .' It was Phyllis, who else?

The ice melted, but I only said, 'Oh good, I thought she would be okay.' When I saw television pictures of Tiananmen Square it really did look as if nothing had happened.

The journalist had asked Sue, 'What do you think of what's happened in Tiananmen Square?'

'Well, tell me what has happened and I'll tell you what I think of it,' she said. And that had been the first she had known of it. There were only three students awake in the block and they decided not to wake anyone up but to wait until morning to break the news.

When morning came there were a few burnt-out cars outside the campus and the English students spent the day sitting on the roof looking out over the stunned city: 'We just sat there looking at the campus under a thunderous sky, with a helicopter circling overhead. The day didn't seem to move,' she has told us since.

Sue, her English friend Heidi and the rest of the group from Durham University were taken to the British Embassy where they stayed overnight and were then escorted to the airport to catch a flight to Hong Kong, from where they were to fly home to Gatwick. 'I have never been as pleased to be British as when our plane landed on the runway at Hong Kong airport,' I remember Sue saying to me when she got home. 'I had an incredible sense of relief and suddenly felt safe again.'

While the group of English students were in Hong Kong, TV AM set up a television link with presenter Mike Morris and invited us down to the studios in Manchester. We could see and hear Sue on the screen, but she could only hear us, so our exchange of words was robotic, but we were very grateful for three minutes of communication.

'You're looking well, Sue.'

'I'm looking forward to coming home. I'll see you tomorrow,' she said.

Sue says she remembers Mike Morris telling her that I was in tears, but I don't remember that bit.

Heidi's father, a dentist, was in the TV studio in London and the interview was such an ordeal for him he could hardly speak. I felt so sorry for him. He was obviously so relieved to see his daughter that every time the camera cut to him all he did was show his teeth. The main thing was that Sue managed to give us the flight number and time of arrival at Gatwick.

The Cathay Pacific plane that carried Sue from Beijing to Gatwick was a most welcome sight. I've always been frightened of aeroplanes, but the one that brought my daughter home appeared to me like a giant gentle bird. The arrivals hall was packed with tense parents but as soon as we saw Sue's face everything was back to normal.

'Hello, I'm fine,' she said as her mother grabbed her from the crowd.

Phyllis laughed and said, 'Yes, but I'm not!'

Then Sue and her friend Heidi were whisked off to talk to TV AM. They were very lucid considering the jet-lag factor, but Sue said afterwards that she felt completely detached from the whole situation; it wasn't about her and she had made no close personal Chinese friends, but she felt sad for the nation.

Sue hasn't talked to us very much about her experience on the night of Tiananmen Square and I'm not sure she would want me to write about it either. She did say that back at the campus at Beijing University they were bringing little children's bloodstained waistcoats back with bullet holes in them. We had kept every newspaper report of the events in Beijing and in that factual way we were better informed than she had been. At home she spent a long time in her room, reading all the newspapers we'd kept for her. It was obviously a very upsetting experience that we couldn't share, but after Sue had spent a couple of weeks in her room with her own thoughts we gave her the traditional family support line, otherwise known as a kick up the bum, by saying, 'If you're not going to do anything with that horse outside we're going to sell it.'

Sue got the message and got on with her life. She continued her studies at Durham University for a further two years and graduated with a joint honours degree in Chinese and Business Studies. No job opportunities were afforded her in Britain so she took a teaching post in Kagoshima, partly to earn some money and partly to improve her Japanese, which she had studied at subsidiary level at Durham. She then came back from Japan via the rest of the world, travelling on the Trans-Siberian railway, stopping off for picnics in Mongolia and Azerbaijan and having afternoon tea with Mum in Moscow. I love it; to think that at her age I was a travelling man simply by virtue of tripping from Chester to Accrington at weekends. Still, I feel I'm lucky to earn a living by making people laugh and taking their minds off weekday worries with a good game show.

Sue came back from Japan, returned to Durham to do a bit of lecturing and a PhD course. Three months into the course the prospect of spending three more years in the sheltered world of academia began to daunt her. She casually dropped a CV on what turned out to be a very important person's desk and one year later, after a series of searching interviews, was fortunate enough to land a job on the Japanese desk of a highly prestigious merchant bank in the city. So at the time of going to press Sue is telephoning her way through life and earning a respectable salary. It has only taken her twenty-four years to contribute in any way to the Bowen household. Her brother had been contributing years before her. We don't mind really, as long as between them they earn enough to keep us in our dotage. We would prefer to by-pass the broom cupboard and go straight into the main ward with the rest of them, just like my dad.

24

Stormy Passage

I've heard it said that every man believes in heredity until his son makes a fool of himself. I would also say that a son rarely acknowledges what he's inherited until he is forty years old. This chapter is one of self-analysis and self-criticism or appraisal, one which addresses my relationship with my son. My awareness of this relationship, or indeed lack of it, has been heightened by the writing of this autobiography. What it has done is make me see myself through a larger window, shedding more light on all my imperfections and short-comings. In 1992 I was made vividly aware that I was the father of an eighteen-year-old son called Peter. A bit late in the day!

Pete's A-level results signalled that he had completely and suddenly lost direction. His projected grades were two Bs and a C. He got two Ds and an also-ran. He had been offered conditional places at Durham and at Nottingham, and now he was scrambling to get in anywhere. I hit the roof and discovered that he had been going to raves when I thought he'd been working, but as raves seemed to be the accepted teenage leisure activity there was no point in trying to veto them while he was at university. He would integrate into student life in his own way.

When Pete took up his place at the Carlisle campus of the

University of Northumbria, we made sure he had a car and a house. Four months later that seemed like a major mistake, when we discovered he had been involved in the drug scene for some time. He had a cheap base and a means of transport: all he needed to set him on the road to total destruction. Pete's house was used for parties, his car was used to ferry people to raves and away-days, and by the end of the first term he knew things had got out of hand both on the work front and the party front. So he dropped out of Carlisle and came home to Station House. University was not to be the life for him.

Christmas 1992 was the most unhappy Christmas the four of us had ever spent together. Pete and I handled the problem by not speaking to each other. Sue was at home, listening to Pete. Phyllis was listening to Pete and me. Both were forced into playing messengers of gloom. It was Sue who explained to me that Pete's involvement with drugs had left him hundreds of pounds in debt to a supplier and that he was hiding from the person he owed money to. We all thought that if I paid the debt the whole scenario with drugs would be over because Pete had made it abundantly clear that he was sick of the hassle and wanted to leave behind the mess he'd got himself into and make a new start.

A local forester friend, Dave, gave Pete a job, from eight in the morning until six at night, chopping and felling trees, giving him a chance to get his head together; it was virtually therapy although he did earn a few quid too.

Sure enough, shortly after Pete's debt was cleared, the police paid us a visit at Station House and said, 'We're sorry to have to come here, Jim. We've tried to keep this away from you but Pete isn't at his Carlisle address and we need to speak to him.'

Pete was out working with Dave, so Phyllis and the plain-clothes officers went their separate ways to find him at one of the forestry sites.

When he came home the police searched his room and found pieces of paper with lists of names on them. They confronted Pete with the lists, which added to the evidence already being assembled by the police inquiry.

'What exactly are these names about? Are you dealing in drugs?' I said.

Pete told me that he wasn't dealing, but that a group of friends took it in turns to buy ecstasy for each other. He described the whole thing as no more than a routine that all his friends knew about, acknowledged even by those who didn't take drugs. However, this did not in any way deflect the policemen from their task.

'We have to take Pete in for questioning,' said one of the officers. 'We are allowed to keep him there for up to twenty-four hours.'

'That's no problem as far as I'm concerned,' I told the police. 'You can keep him in as long as it takes to get this problem sorted out because we don't have the experience to do it ourselves. Keep him there for three months and send me the bill for the food. As long as it takes; I don't mind.'

'He can have a solicitor there while we take a statement,' said the plain-clothes officer.

'Why should that be necessary?' I asked. 'You're going to be fair with him, aren't you?'

'Of course.'

'Well I'm not having a solicitor or a social worker there on my say so. He'll tell you what he has to tell you. I think you'll find he's reached the stage where he wants to tell the truth.'

The police kept him at the station for more than twenty-four hours because there was a lot of work to go through. That night must have been an ordeal for Pete. The detective constable phoned the next day and said, 'He's been sent home with a caution, but we're a bit concerned about the chef here because Pete says he actually enjoyed his breakfast!' So Pete may have been directly responsible for the dismissal of a certain prison chef in Cumbria, accused of making a very enjoyable breakfast.

When Pete came home from the police station he said he had had the best night's sleep he'd had for months, so we could see a bit of light at the end of the tunnel. Then a phone call put out the light again . . .

The call came when I was on a train on my way down to London: 'Your son has been reported for buying ecstasy. We've got his name, we've got photographs of him and apparently he has been involved in the rave scene for some time.' It was Charlie Yates of the *Sun* who brought home to me the truth, beyond my worst fears, about my son's life as a student in Carlisle and, I realized to my horror, that this involvement with the drugs scene had probably been established when he was still at school.

'You can talk to us or not, but the story is going to come out anyway. If you don't want to do it, we'll have to take what our witness says and print it,' Charlie Yates explained. 'You have a high profile on family television; you are news and, I'm afraid, so are your family.'

The possibility of a newspaper story had been hanging over us since Christmas, so Phyllis and I had already talked about what we would do. Charlie Yates and I discussed it at length and decided that the best way forward for all concerned was to bury the whole issue in one fell swoop by letting the *Sun* take the story exclusively. And, as Charlie said, 'Do a positive, constructive, forward-thinking article on how drugs can affect even the most stable of households.

'Trust me, and be up front,' he said.

Phyllis and I now knew the awful extent of the drugs problem among our youngsters. And, although this would be very hard for our family, we knew others would benefit from such a story.

'Right,' I said. 'You've got it, Charlie.'

How long had this been going on, I asked myself? Surely we couldn't have missed such obvious signs. The fact is we did.

I'd never guessed that Pete had been involved with drugs at all. Truth to tell, he embarked on this wayward track when he was in the fifth year at Lancaster Boys' Grammar School, going to raves, at first quite innocently, enjoying the friendly atmosphere and the music. It's the old adage: one thing led to another. And the *Sun* had been informed of his activities during his first term at the Carlisle campus of the University of Northumbria. We had got it wrong. But, luckily, as it turned out, it wasn't too late to start getting it right.

I didn't discuss with Pete the decision to do the article with the *Sun*. It was my decision, and I was seeking a way to close the distressing episode once and for all, with as positive an outcome as possible for all concerned, not least of all the *Sun* readers.

An eighteen-year-old is old enough to vote a prime minister into power, so why should parents say, 'Where have you been?' when he arrives home for lunch having left the previous evening? Well, we did, as it happens, but still the subtle warning signs of a young life going out of control only became clear in retrospect.

How could I have missed a situation like this? My son had had a problem and I'd simply assumed that his upbringing would stand him in good stead to resist any negative temptations or pressures from his peers. I had been a teacher and seen how even the best parental will in the world can be overthrown by peer pressure. I knew Pete had something to sort out between his ears, just as I'd had to do at his age, but I had no idea he had been meddling with mind-changing chemicals.

I think Pete disappointed me less than I disappointed my dad when I failed my GCEs, because we confronted the problem together and now he's working hard to pay off his debt. The worst thing for me is that, when you realize that your son has been deceiving you for eighteen months, the trust is damaged. Because of his lifestyle he couldn't tell us the truth about anything he was doing, but you can't wave a wand to re-establish that trust.

Now Pete is working at building the independence to make his own life. He enjoys home life, Mum's cooking and is working hard. Of course, we agonize over how we might have helped him to find himself a bit more quickly. I often think I should have anticipated the problem or stopped him from going to all those raves, but when you live in a village and all your friends are in the nearest town ten miles away, you want to be out with them, not with the thirteen-year-olds and the limited social life of the village. That's why he got his car. We were able to afford to get him one and we didn't regard that as spoiling him.

Charlie Yates wrote two superb articles and gave me a fair amount of editorial control. It was a front-page story, which meant that Pete was subjected to unwanted publicity but he understood that this was the price he was having to pay for his two years of indiscretion. I was proud of the way he handled the difficult situation of walking down the village street, even though it was some time before he could raise his head. I can say he's now looking where he's going.

The *Sun* also talked to the police in Cumbria to check that their report would not damage official investigations. The journalists displayed commendable tact and diplomacy.

A few weeks later the Calcott Report came out with ideas of trying to gag the press. Calcott might as well sit in a room with Lord Longford and Wedgie Benn; he's in a world of idealists, a man who is not of this earth. Say what you like about the tabloids, there is a valid place for them in the British way of life. Never gag the media – you can't do it because we'd lose television documentaries and investigative journalism at its best. I've always had good relations with the press, even though there are times when I'd like to put them all in a box and shove them underground for a month. You can't change the rules. When I was first on TV I wanted publicity and now I was experiencing the other side of the coin.

After the story came out, Charlie rang me to say, 'The feedback we got was tremendous.'

It's at times like this, when the tide has seemed against me, that the reaction from fans can be a great source of consolation. As a result of having had many letters from viewers, both giving and asking advice about our specific situation and the rave scene, I am sure we were right to be as upfront about the whole painful episode as we were. Almost without exception the letters we received were cries for help or thanks for the warning or wished us good luck for the future.

25

Calmer Waters

As soon as the last rope is released on the *QE2* Phyllis can forget about all land events and float away. When we are at home she seems to carry the details of my diary in her head, but she has the facility to forget all about domestic matters as soon as the ship has pulled a few yards away from the dock at Southampton. For me it's my favourite brand of working holiday and at this stage of my life the highlight of my year. I just wish it would pull in at Heysham and then I could hop on more often.

On board the *QE2* my cabaret act is vetted by an official from, I presume, a moral standpoint, which rendered my first ever performance in the Double Down room a little more sedate than usual. On my first night I was worried sick – fine if I did well, but if you die on your backside on the first night of a cruise, you've got ten more days on board to spend avoiding the rest of the passengers. You can't drive out of town because you're in the middle of the Bay of Biscay! And doing your first show on the fifth night is just as taxing, because you then get four long nights waiting in a huge floating dressing-room.

The Double Down – the name has since changed to the Grand Lounge – is a large, gracious, long room where cabarets are held for large, very gracious, well-wedged audiences. Fortunately, I quickly found that a bit of naughtiness and a lot of laughter are just as infectious on a cruise liner as they were at the Ocean Edge Caravan Park twenty years ago. And, even better, when I wandered into the Theatre Bar I discovered one of the ship's bands – Colin Bryant and the Hot Rhythm Orchestra (fondly known as the HRO).

So, when the cruise Director said he would like to have me back to work on the *QE2* again, I asked if I would be able to work with the HRO, which would mean I might be allowed to take out my trumpet! Also it would take the pressure off having to wait for the daunting experience of doing my cabaret act in the Grand Lounge.

The bandleader Colin Bryant, a superb clarinet player, is loath to let anyone join in with his band because volunteers almost invariably disrupt rather than enhance the band's performance. Nevertheless, he gave me a try and my singing and trumpet-playing seemed to work very well and now I'm almost resident with the band. Needless to say they don't admit to my being a member of the HRO. And who can blame them!

One of my most enjoyable trips was the cruise with the Loud Purr. On the ship's first voyage after a £90 million refit in Bremerhaven there came to pass a slight but permanent vibration. It wasn't a big problem, but if you had paid £5,000 for a holiday, which I hadn't, it wasn't nice. And it was particularly not nice for the Captain, Alan Bennell (whom we sadly lost at a tragically early age). Now the Captain normally goes out on the bridge only in cases of fierce gales, fog or any unusual threat to the ship, and for the rest of the time lives like the Lord Mayor of Floating City. On the cruise with the Loud Purr he had to ensure that all passengers' queries about the vibrations were dealt with diplomatically. The Captain is not just the front man because even though most of his time is spent in dress uniform, shaking hands and giving cocktail parties, he is also ultimately responsible for the course followed by the ship to reach its destination.

Towards the end of the week of the Loud Purr trip, Alan

Bennell told me, 'The staff have had a hard time this week. The noise is worst in their quarters and they have had to do a lot of explaining to passengers. Could you do a special show for them on Friday, Jim, to cheer them up?'

'I'd love to,' I replied. 'And I suppose if it's for the staff I won't be passed through the censors . . .'

Roger de Courcey was also to perform in the show with Nookie Bear and we knew we were going to have a great night. The Grand Lounge was to be closed late on Friday evening and only the staff allowed in for their exclusive cabaret. It was to be a no-holds-barred, anything-goes evening. I could hardly wait.

The HRO and I were packing the Theatre Bar every night and I kept telling the audiences, 'Now please remember, ladies and gentlemen, that you must *not* go into the Grand Lounge late on Friday night. It closes at midnight and there's a show for the crew which will be very naughty. You mustn't go in there, you might be offended by the performance.'

When the night came I nipped out from backstage to take a peek into the Grand Lounge and saw about 800 crew members sitting comfortably on the floor with their six-packs of beer, as planned. The galleria of shopping malls high above the audience was also packed with people, but they were definitely not crew, as I recognized some of the frocks and suits from the Theatre Bar.

I said to Alan, 'I think you'd better go out there and check the audience to make sure there are no passengers in the vicinity. We wouldn't want *QE2* passengers listening to the sort of thing that will get the ship a bad name.' (Max Miller, 1935.)

He went out, came back to me and said, 'I see no passengers.'

'Alan, there's got to be nearly a thousand up there on the balconies. They're all settling down to watch and they're going to get their eyes opened if they stay there,' I warned him.

'Sorry,' said Captain Alan. 'I can't see any passengers at all.' Talk about Nelson turning a blind eye!

What a great show it was! A bit strong, but a great two-hour show with one of the biggest and best audiences I've ever set eyes on.

I saw the Captain the following day and asked him if he'd had any response. 'There were a few letters on my desk this morning,' said Captain Alan. 'But they're not there now.' What a fine man he was.

Tony Green was also with me on the Loud Purr trip and one evening he decided to liven up dinner by talking to two ladies from Huddersfield whose main topic of discussion had been who was feeding what to their cats while they were on holiday. The ship had a very slight list, loosely connected with the Purr and easy to notice if you looked at the coffee in your cup. Tony pointed out the lean of the ship to the ladies and explained, 'You see how the view of the sea is at different levels on each side of the ship?' The ladies looked and nodded. 'Well, that's because the crew are all up on the starboard deck having an angling competition. If you feel a sudden judder in the night, that means that one of the crew has caught something very big. They often fish all night. They sleep in the lifeboats at the side, you know, so they can keep their rods in the water.'

'Oh, do the crew really sleep in those little boats?' the Huddersfield ladies exclaimed.

'Where else?' replied Tony. 'Though most nights they go home.'

A 68,000-ton ship travelling at thirty knots in the Bay of Biscay is very fast for a city. And sometimes common sense in conversation aboard a cruise liner evaporates!

In 1993 working on the *QE2* gave me the opportunity of meeting the great Max Bygraves, with whom I'd never worked before. Normally I don't worry too much about who else is performing on board ship as long as the HRO are there, but

seeing Max in action was not to be missed. The Grand
Lounge was the venue where he was to appear – the room I
feared and dreaded was to be captured with all its human
content by a man whose charisma is amazing.

Anyone who can get away with singing a song for forty years
about two toothbrushes sharing the same toothpaste has to
have something special. And he has. He had sane people
singing along, too; a thousand people who had paid thousands
of pounds to be there were singing this song about pink and
blue toothbrushes getting married. When will people ever
learn that behaviour aboard a great ship is not to be admitted
to on dry land? Or was it just the magic of Max?

I remember his opening lines about Captain Robin
Woodall: 'You know the Captain's a lot happier with this ship
than his last one – the *Torrey Canyon*.'

Roars of laughter. Robin Woodall had been Captain in an
unfortunate incident. One incident in nearly thirty years
driving floating cities surely must be allowed. Robin Woodall
happened to be Captain at the time the *QE2* ran aground on
Martha's Vineyard. It doesn't matter whose fault it was,
because poor Robin bore the ultimate responsibility as master
of the ship. He's an impressive, statuesque man, regarded by
his fellow seamen as the best. I suppose you don't get to be
captain of the world's greatest ship unless you're something
special.

Robin heard Max's gag and loved it, in fact most of the
comedians in the Theatre Bar spend a lot of time reassuring
the audience about our sobering up the captain during the
day in order that we might get somewhere near our intended
destination at a time to be announced. The Captain hears of
it all – he is fully aware of *everything* that goes on aboard the
QE2.

A couple of years ago I was in full flow in the Theatre Bar
on our way to the Midnight Sun, giving full vent to the
incompetence of our Captain, extolling his weaknesses, i.e.
wine, women and wine, expressing severe doubts about our
safe return to the UK, when the whole audience went deathly

silent. Who should be leaning round the bar but the ship's master. There was an embarrassed hush as the Captain walked up to me, whispered sweet nothings in my ear, then strode out of the bar. Neither the audience nor you, dear reader, will ever know what he said to me. We get married next Thursday.

My weeks afloat with the HRO have spanned ten years now and, because jazz and their talent travels so well, I can sometimes persuade them to come and play a couple of gigs at celebrated venues like my local pub, the Redwell Inn.

I've always wanted a nice trumpet for myself, even though I may never ever do justice to one. So I had a hand-crafted, all-singing, all-dancing, gleaming one made as a birthday treat to myself by a group of lunatics based in Luton. Sterling Musical Instruments Ltd made me a superb instrument and when I showed it to Dave Davis, trumpet player of the HRO, what do you think he said?

'Well, Jim, it's like giving a Ferrari to someone who hasn't passed his driving test.' How kind.

And so my dream of trumpet-playing takes me back to the old man I worked with on the dustbins, who said, 'We're only here for a bloody weekend.' Consequently engraved on my Luton-made hand-crafted trumpet are the words, 'It's not a rehearsal.'

We only go this way once and I'm still aiming to make the most of it. My greatest ambition, apart from waking up tomorrow with Phyllis, is to have ten years as good as the last ten and improve my trumpet-playing. I'd like nothing more than to be able to nip down to the Redwell and play requests for my friends. So I've booked some lessons in my pulpit, and to the lady who wrote and complained about its use as a bar in Station House, having read a little about it in a magazine, I'd like to say there will be *no hymns* played during those lessons.

Another prized possession of mine which has been given

pride of place in the Redwell is a handsome sculpted terracotta plaque in the shape of a Nori brick cradled in two hands, with a dart embedded in the brick! This was presented to me when I went back to the Nori brickworks to do a documentary about my roots, thirty-five years after working there as a student.

'You'll see some changes now, Jim,' said the foreman.

I was expecting a clinic by comparison to my memories of the place in 1955. Well, the environmentalists had been in with their vacuum cleaners, there were a lot of new screens, modern technology had been employed in the firing system, and superficially things did look nearer to the twentieth century.

'Yes, I can see a difference,' I told the foreman after my guided tour. 'The bricks are moving more quickly, but it's still a mucky madhouse. The atmosphere is the same; it still breeds great characters. You still need a lot of bottle to work here. Fundamentally nothing has changed; we're dealing with clay, dust, soot and fire. Without these elements, you ain't making no bricks.'

'Eh, Jim! Do you remember 1957? When we did four hours' overtime for three nights to get you a bit extra for your honeymoon?' Yes, one of the lads I had worked with in my student days was still working there.

We reminisced about Frannie Willesey and the brave Methodist preacher and some of the other nutters who had worked with us.

The gift of the beautiful plaque was typical of all that Accrington brickworks meant to me. Hard work, humour, care, attention to detail, and that element of inventiveness that comes from working in dire circumstances. If anything ever were to remind me of where I came from, surely it was that. There was my dad, his basin of stew, the walk up the hill with my mum, my own promotion to dinner deliverer. And also it serves to remind me of the value of human life and endeavour along with all its attendant skills, at whatever academic or industrial level.

Thank you Nori, thank you trumpet, thank you Phyllis, thank you Bully. All I ask from life is more of the same please. Whilst writing this book I watched 'The Comedians' twenty years on in a television special for Christmas 1993. Seeing the old gang, sadly a little depleted, made me realize the deep and meaningful significance of gaining wrinkles. The older you get, the more you must find to laugh about. Lucky the person whose wrinkles are laughter lines.

The general practice in our business at the end of the performance is to walk off stage to thunderous applause and laughter, as the band plays you away with the full expectation of playing you back on stage to do a bit more. The performer then returns by popular demand to do that bit extra. This comes as no surprise because the performer knows he has every intention of coming back to do a well-rehearsed, tried-and-tested climactic encore, planned to leave the audience in an increased state of frenzy. These are called false tabs.

I don't do that, and I'll tell you why. I'm not of the school of the climactic encore; I've never been keen on false tabs. As a result of rarely experiencing a strong call for my return after my initial departure, I'd rather not risk false tabs. I've had so many nights waiting to be called back that I don't risk it any more. When I go, I go for good.

But now, as the curtains draw on this book, I am able to say that I hope you have enjoyed it. This is not a live performance and my audience is one, that's you, the reader. So I can give you the choice of a little bit extra. If you would like to read on, please continue with the next chapter. It may be the last. Otherwise, you can of course close the book now and put it wherever you like. For once I'm doing a false tab.

26

False Tabs

I always used to believe that it was verging on the arrogant and self-indulgent to write an autobiography and I've certainly never felt that anyone would want to know about what really makes me tick. It's a 'We're not worthy' situation. But I think I've had a story to tell you and it's meant as a kind of thank you to all the millions of you who have watched 'Bullseye' over the years, lived with us through our shortcomings and mistakes and, we like to think, enjoyed our success with us. You don't invite us into your front rooms, we just appear.

I have to tell you that writing this book has been rather like looking at a radar scanner. It has shown me exactly where I am on my journey in relation to other ships.

Looking at videos and old photographs of what I used to be has enhanced my appreciation of the present and helped me to see my path forward. Writing about the past has heightened my awareness of where I come from and will probably help me to reach many decisions in the future. I want to be able to give up the business and know when it is time to do so. I like to think I would know when to let go. I did a radio show once with Tommy Trinder when he was in a wheelchair. Tommy was one of the all-time greats and I knew what fantastic timing and discipline he'd had; I saw it gone. I felt saddened.

If, like me, you're lucky enough to enjoy earning your daily bread, it's important to keep it in perspective. I've always tried to make sure that the work needs me more than I need the work. Anyone who lives to work rather than works to live I think has a problem. Some people are past their sell-by date at forty-five because between their ears they are bitter and they think they have missed the boat through no fault of their own. This affects their confidence, attitude and general behaviour. The odd one or two of those whom I know as comics, but would never name, are among my Obliterati. They achieve nothing, create little and destroy a lot.

When a comic goes on stage and gets a wave of laughter coming back at him, it is like a drug. My job is to make people laugh – simple as that – but there are comics who go on stage on their own terms and not to benefit the audience but their own ego and they will stay on there for ever.

I know my place. I'd rather close the first half of a show than top the bill. I am not a room-filler, but there again I'm not as expensive as a room-filler and I like to think, in my own little tinpot way, that I'm a good comic, good value for money, and the chances are that my diary will never be completely empty.

The adrenalin that accompanies the sound of laughter has always been a driving force in my life. But I don't want it to take me over completely; I don't need to own the laughs, I enjoy sharing them. You see, it's not *my* laughter, it's yours. There are nights that I would prefer to take Phyllis out for a drink than go on stage, but it's a blessing to be able to go out there and get laughter on demand when I need it. And it would be quite nice to continue to switch on the adrenalin tap for a few more years, not because I've got a bank manager saying I've got to do it but because I feel like it.

There's never been a lack of laughter in my life for any length of time, so I've never had the time to develop withdrawal symptoms. But when the 'phone don't ring no more' I hope I can come to terms with the situation. I would quite like to know that it's over without an undertaker telling me so. And who knows, if there isn't another book to write, I might find time for some physical exercise – a spot of swimming perhaps, or maybe a walk in the Lakes, or more frequent walks to the car. But if anyone ever sees me on a golf course, please call a doctor.

This time I'm definitely signing off. Cue the band! Thank you and good night.

Was that all right, Phyllis?